LUCAS WENNERSTEN

Crossing the 49th Parallel

A Retirement Planning Guide for Moving Across the Canada–U.S. Border

First edition

This book was professionally typeset on Reedsy.
Find out more at reedsy.com

Contents

Foreword

This book is more than a guide. It is a labor of love, thoughtfully crafted and carefully curated by my dear husband, Lucas.

The seed for *Crossing the 49th Parallel* was planted during the first few months of our family's move to Toronto. Surrounded by the charm of the city and the quiet majesty of rural Canada, we were drawn in completely. What began as a new chapter in our lives quickly became a place we could call home.

Lucas began writing this book in the middle of what most would consider a storm: starting a demanding new job, welcoming our fourth and youngest child (our sweet "Canadian anchor baby"), enduring the uncertainty of the COVID-19 pandemic, and preparing for the grueling Chartered Financial Analyst exams. Yet somehow, he still carved out time for this project quietly, faithfully, and relentlessly.

I've watched him pour his whole self into every page, not just for the benefit of others navigating the same cross-border complexities we once faced, but as a gift to our children. This book is part of his legacy one that we hope our four children will one day cherish and draw from as they grow into the kind, principled, and hard-working individuals their father inspires them to be.

To know Lucas is to know someone deeply loyal, humbly brilliant, and steadfast in all he does. This book reflects not only his expertise, but his integrity. It stands as a testament to his love for his family, his profession, and the countless individuals seeking clarity in the midst of financial and emotional transitions.

May this guide offer you more than just direction. May it offer you peace, purpose, and the same sense of home we found when we crossed the 49th parallel.

With love and admiration,

Shakorah Wennersten

1

Introduction

"*As in all successful ventures, the foundation of a good retirement is planning.*

— *Earl Nightingale*

Moving across an international border is a huge undertaking. While movers can be hired to take care of most of the physical move, the more difficult part is figuring out how to plan and coordinate your finances going forward. Having a family also complicates things. You will most likely need help from someone who has experienced such a move and knows what challenges and hurdles you can expect.

The most common questions I get from clients are:

- When can I afford to retire?
- How can I reduce my taxes?
- When should I take Social Security (SS), Canada Pension Plan (CPP), and Old Age Security (OAS) retirement benefits?

The next question is usually: If I do not take my government retirement pensions when I retire, what should I use to live off until I do? Most people who have lived and worked in Canada and the United States will qualify for all three government pension systems: SS, CPP, and OAS. They likely also have savings in Registered Retirement Savings Plans (RRSPs), 401(k)s, 403(b)s, Individual Retirement Accounts (IRAs), pensions, and other types of tax-deferred retirement savings plans. They may also have taxable savings and investments in both countries, and in both currencies. Planning around the decision of when to take government retirement pension benefits, and when to distribute funds from each account, is what I call retirement cash-flow sequencing. This is an area that can be quite complex for people living a Canada-U.S. lifestyle.

This book is not intended to answer all your Canada-U.S. financial planning questions. It focuses on retirement planning. I also touch on several other topics as they relate to retirement, cash flow, or taxes. You may notice that I skim over some things. I do this because I want this book to be as easy to understand as possible, which means I do not want to discuss things in depth that are not important for retirement planning.

Benefit amounts, income thresholds, and contribution limits are usually indexed and change as often as quarterly. The numbers used in this book will likely be outdated by the time it is published. So, do not use this book as an information source for such things; you can search for those details on the internet and find updated amounts.

My objective is to make you aware of concepts and possibilities, not solve your individual issues. There is a lot to remember here, so certain numbers and concepts are repeated throughout the book to help you make sense of things as you go, rather than having to constantly reference other areas of the book.

When using the term "Canada-U.S. lifestyle", I am not talking about Snow-birds or Sunbirds. Snowbirds are people from Canada, or the northern states such as Minnesota or Wisconsin, who spend the winter months in southern states like Florida or Arizona. Sunbirds are from the southern U.S. and do the opposite: spend the summer in Canada or northern U.S. While they do spend time in both countries as visitors, their financial lives are not made significantly more complicated as they are vacationing when they are away from their home country. Snowbirds and Sunbirds have not changed their tax residency, worked away from their home country, built government benefits or other retirement savings away from home, or gained legal immigration status elsewhere. These are things that complicate your financial life.

So, what should be considered when living a cross-border lifestyle? The typical Canada-U.S. financial plan should include sections on immigration planning, customs planning, cash-flow planning, cross-border tax planning, retirement planning, risk management, education planning, estate planning, and investment planning. This book has a narrow focus but will also incorporate different aspects of many of the financial planning areas because they all work together, affect each other, and should be coordinated. For example, in a cross-border context, your immigration status is the foundation for tax planning, cash-flow planning, retirement planning, investment management, education planning and estate planning. Planning in all these areas must be updated once your immigration status changes.

The problem with doing your own financial planning in a cross-border context is you may not know the right questions to ask. All the information I am going to share with you is available in various other places. It will take time and effort to find the resources you need, decipher what is applicable to your situation, and organize the information. Even if you have a thorough understanding of your home country's financial system, it takes years to learn the financial system of another country, let alone the international treaties and agreements that will help to alleviate some of the more burdensome aspects of living a cross-border lifestyle. For example, in this book I will be talking about two agreements: the Canada-U.S. Tax Treaty and the Social Security Totalization Agreement. The financial systems of Canada and the U.S. are similar in many ways but quite different in others. These two agreements dictate how to treat differences between the two countries' taxation and government benefits.

For those who are younger, single, or have not built substantial assets in their home country, a move across the Canada-U.S. border will be much simpler. If you have done your research and have enough knowledge to make a cross-border move on your own, then you should do it. There is no reason to pay someone to tell you things you already know. But if you have significant assets on both sides of the border, income streams from both countries, or business interests in both countries, I recommend you consult a professional, because every situation is more complex than it seems. The cost of making a mistake can be significant.

The exchange rate may be difficult to understand for someone who is new to a cross-border lifestyle. For example, an exchange rate of 0.8 USD/CAD or 1.25 CAD/USD is used when converting numbers in this book. When reading currency conversion quotes, the last currency is the base currency and always represents $1 in that currency. Another way of writing the quote above would be $0.8 USD converts to $1 CAD, or $1.25 CAD converts to $1 USD.

Every family is unique, and every situation is different. My goal in this book is not to provide everyone with a personalized financial plan or distribution roadmap. I am going to point out the considerations that should be made and share with you how I think through these issues as a planner. We will examine a variety of factors that should be considered before making these tough decisions. Many people can handle the decision-making process on their own. Others will need assistance, do not want to spend the time figuring it out, or do not feel equipped to make these decisions on their own. If you are one of these people, you should hire a professional, because these decisions will affect your financial health in your golden years, and the inheritance left to your heirs.

2

Social Security (SS)

We can never insure 100% of the population against 100% of the hazards and vicissitudes of life but have tried to frame a law which will give some measure of protection to the average citizen and to his family against the loss of a job and against poverty-ridden old age.

Franklin D. Roosevelt

Social Security is the U.S. federal insurance program that provides benefits to people of retirement age, their spouses, survivors, or those who are disabled. Social Security Retirement benefits are the primary source of income for most retired Americans. Generally, 40 quarters of work history with a minimum annual income of $7,240 (2025) is required to qualify for SS retirement benefits ($1,810 per quarter or $603.33 per month)[1]. You can start taking your benefits as early as age 62 or as late as age 70.

People born prior to 1937 have a full retirement age (FRA) of 65. The FRA then increases by two months for each birth year group, eventually reaching 67 for those who are born in 1960 or later. If this group of retirees starts taking their benefits before age 67, there will be a reduction in their benefits of approximately 6% per year (30% at age 62). If they delay receiving benefits until after age 67, they will increase those benefits by 8% per year[2] (24% at age 70)[3].

The Social Security Administration (SSA) provides an annual benefit statement complete with estimated benefits for those who currently qualify for benefits through their U.S. work history. If you do not have 40 quarters (10 years) of work history, your SS statement will show your work history but will not include a benefit estimate. As I will discuss later, many Canadians who work in the U.S. for fewer than 10 years will qualify for SS benefits but will not be able to get a benefit estimate from the SSA, which can make retirement planning more difficult.

The estimate on the SS statement assumes you work until you begin taking benefits. This is important to remember if there is a gap between when you retire and when you begin taking benefits (as is often the case). Your actual benefit may be slightly lower than the estimate, depending on your work

---

[1] https://www.ssa.gov/benefits/retirement/planner/credits.html

[2] https://www.ssa.gov/benefits/retirement/planner/delayret.html

[3] https://www.ssa.gov/benefits/retirement/planner/agereduction.html

history and if any years are being disregarded.

Everyone should set up an online profile at www.ssa.gov and check their SS benefit statement annually to ensure that their U.S. earnings are recorded accurately. If you will be retiring before taking your SS benefit, use the SSA's online retirement benefit calculator[4] for a more accurate benefit estimate.

If you will not be able to get an estimate because you did not work in the U.S. for 10 years, you can use the online benefit calculator to generate an estimate. You will need to enter 10 years of earnings history for the calculator to generate a benefit. Enter the minimum annual earnings amount for any missing years so that you can enter a full 10 years of history.

You don't want to enter more income into the calculator than the amount you really earned, so any phantom income you entered to complete the 10-year history should be deducted approximately equally from any real earnings history that you have. You should deduct a little extra to be safe. This will not be accurate but will give you some idea of what your benefit may be.

If you are currently married for at least one year, or if you were previously married for at least 10 years, and you do not have enough SS credits to qualify for your own retirement benefit, you may be able to receive a spousal benefit[5]. Those who have been married multiple times will receive the spousal benefit from whichever former spouse has the highest SS benefit. However, if you are currently married, you can only qualify for spousal benefits based on your current spouse's earnings record.

To qualify for spousal benefits, you must be:

- At least 62 years of age; or

---

[4] https://www.ssa.gov/benefits/retirement/planner/AnypiaApplet.html

[5] https://www.forbes.com/advisor/retirement/social-security-spousal-benefits/

- Any age if caring for a child who is younger than age 16 or disabled and is entitled to receive benefits on your spouse's record[6].

The maximum spousal benefit is one half of the FRA benefit of the qualifying spouse. In other words, if one spouse has a benefit that is more than double the benefit of the other spouse, the spouse with the lower benefit will also receive a spousal benefit. If both spouses take their benefits at their full retirement age, the combined spousal benefit will be half the amount the higher-earning spouse receives.

For example, Jack and Rebecca are married and the same age. Jack is eligible for a SS retirement benefit of $3,000 USD per month at his FRA of 67. Rebecca's retirement benefit is only $1,000 per month at her FRA of 67. Jack and Rebecca both apply for benefits at age 67. Jack will receive his benefit of $3,000 per month. Rebecca will receive her benefit of $1,000 per month plus a spousal benefit of $500 per month for a total benefit of $1,500 per month.

If Jack and Rebecca both wait until age 70 to claim benefits, Jack will receive a higher benefit for waiting. Rebecca's spousal benefit will still total $1,500 (half of the FRA benefit of Jack), not half of the increased benefit Jack receives for waiting until 70. Spousal benefits do not increase for delaying past the FRA; you just miss out on payments you were eligible to receive. If Rebecca takes spousal benefits before FRA, they will decrease like retirement benefits but at a different rate[7]. You will receive the maximum spousal benefit if you wait until your FRA to begin receiving benefits.

If you qualify for your own benefit and a spousal benefit, you do not have to apply separately. The SSA will automatically send you the highest eligible amount. Your benefit will always be paid first. If you are eligible for a larger spousal benefit, the difference will automatically be added to your benefit

---

[6] https://blog.ssa.gov/do-you-qualify-for-social-security-spouses-benefits-2/

[7] https://www.ssa.gov/OACT/quickcalc/spouse.html

to equal the spousal benefit. One important factor is that you cannot begin receiving spousal benefits until the qualifying spouse is also receiving their benefits. The exception to this is if you have been divorced for two consecutive years or longer. In that case, you can apply for benefits as early as age 62 if your ex-spouse qualifies for benefits at that time, even if your former spouse is not yet receiving their benefits.

Primary and spousal benefits at age 62
(benefits based on a $1,000 primary insurance amount)

Year of birth [a]	Normal (or full) retirement age	Number of reduction months [b]	Primary		Spouse	
			Amount	Percent reduction [c]	Amount	Percent reduction [d]
1937 or earlier	65	36	$800	20.00%	$375	25.00%
1938	65 and 2 months	38	791	20.83%	370	25.83%
1939	65 and 4 months	40	783	21.67%	366	26.67%
1940	65 and 6 months	42	775	22.50%	362	27.50%
1941	65 and 8 months	44	766	23.33%	358	28.33%
1942	65 and 10 months	46	758	24.17%	354	29.17%
1943-1954	66	48	750	25.00%	350	30.00%
1955	66 and 2 months	50	741	25.83%	345	30.83%
1956	66 and 4 months	52	733	26.67%	341	31.67%
1957	66 and 6 months	54	725	27.50%	337	32.50%
1958	66 and 8 months	56	716	28.33%	333	33.33%
1959	66 and 10 months	58	708	29.17%	329	34.17%
1960 and later	67	60	700	30.00%	325	35.00%

[a] If you are born on January 1, use the prior year of birth.

[b] Applies only if you are born on the 2nd of the month; otherwise the number of reduction months is one less than the number shown.

[c] Reduction applied to primary insurance amount ($1,000 in this example). The percentage reduction is 5/9 of 1% per month for the first 36 months and 5/12 of 1% for each additional month.

In this example, Jack and Rebecca unfortunately divorce before retirement. Rebecca wants to retire early but Jack is determined to work for as long as possible. If they were still married, Rebecca would not be able to receive her spousal benefit until Jack was also receiving his retirement benefit. She could still initiate her own benefit ($1,000 per month in our earlier example), but the spousal benefit would not start until Jack was also receiving benefits. Once they are divorced for two years and Rebecca is at least 62 years of age, Rebecca's spousal benefit can begin (total benefit of $1,500, as in our earlier example) even though Jack has not applied for his retirement benefit.

The decision about when Jack and Rebecca should take their SS benefits is easier if Jack is at least three years older than Rebecca. If Jack starts taking his benefits at age 70 and Rebecca takes hers from age 67, or her FRA, this will maximize both of their benefits. The decision becomes more difficult if Jack is younger than Rebecca. If Jack is three years younger than Rebecca, he would not want to start taking his SS benefits at age 64 when Rebecca's benefits are maximized. Also, if Jack waits until age 70, Rebecca will be 73 and will have missed out on six years of benefit payments, worth $72,000.

Federally, the first 15% of your SS benefits are tax-free, with 50% taxable if your Modified Adjusted Gross Income (MAGI) is between $25,000 and $34,000 for individuals, and $32,000 and $44,000 for married couples filing jointly. 85% of the benefit is taxable for individuals with MAGI above $34,000, or joint filers with MAGI above $44,000[8]. If you live in Colorado, Connecticut, Kansas, Minnesota, Montana, New Mexico, Rhode Island, Utah, or Vermont, contact your state tax agency for details on how benefits in your home state are taxed[9].

According to the Centers for Disease Control and Prevention (CDC), the average statistical life expectancy is 78.[10] Life expectancies vary by gender and nationality and are extended each additional year you are alive. The decision on when to start taking SS benefits is often viewed in terms of a "breakeven" age. In other words, how long do you need to live to make it beneficial to wait past age 62 to initiate your retirement benefit?

To calculate your breakeven age, use your SS statement to determine the difference between your FRA benefit and your age 70 benefit. Next calculate

---

[8] https://www.irs.gov/newsroom/irs-reminds-taxpayers-their-social-security-benefits-may-be-taxable

[9] https://www.nerdwallet.com/article/investing/social-security/which-states-tax-social-security-benefits?msockid=26345d234a1d6aec072f49904b996bcc

[10] https://www.cdc.gov/nchs/data/nvsr/nvsr61/nvsr61_03.pdf

the total amount of payments you would receive between FRA and age 70. Then divide the total amount of payments from FRA until age 70 by the difference in benefit between FRA and age 70. This will give you the number of months needed to equalize total payments. Add those months to age 70 and you have your breakeven age.

1. Age 70 benefit − FRA (67) benefit = benefit difference
2. FRA benefit x 36 = missed payments
3. Missed payments/benefit difference = breakeven months
4. 70+ breakeven months = breakeven age

For example, if my FRA is 67 and my retirement benefit is $1,000 per month, my age 70 benefit is $1,240 per month in current dollars ($1,000 x 124%) − a difference of $240. If I began my SS retirement benefits at 67, I will receive $36,000 annually from my 67th birthday until my 70th birthday ($1,000 x 36 months). Accordingly, it will take me 150 months (12½ years) of payments to make up the difference ($36,000/$240).

The breakeven age when taking benefits early versus FRA will be 82½ or earlier. It will get progressively earlier the younger you are when you take benefits. If instead I took my benefit at age 62, I would receive $700 each month for a total of $42,000 in payments before my 67th birthday. It would take me 140 months (11.67 years) to make up the payment difference of $300 . This would make my breakeven age 73 and eight months when taking benefits at age 62 versus 67 . The breakeven age for taking SS benefits at age 62 versus 70 is approximately 80 and five months.

These "breakeven" numbers are a simple cash-flow calculation that does not factor in the opportunity for investment returns over time. In other words, if you are drawing from your investments for income, you are losing out on the future appreciation of the securities you liquidate to provide that income. Another way of looking at it is to analyze what happens if you invest all your SS benefit payments. This may be the case if you take SS at your FRA but continue to work until age 70.

Calculating a breakeven age which includes a return on investment is much more difficult and requires computer software for most. The higher your rate of return, the later your breakeven age will be. It is impossible to accurately predict future investment returns. 8% is a pretty good guaranteed return, which is the annual increase for delaying SS beyond FRA. If you have the funds to support your lifestyle until age 70, you should wait until that age to take your SS benefits.

If you are going to take benefits early, you should take them at 62 or as soon as you retire, whichever is later. The penalty for taking benefits early is smaller than the increase for taking benefits after FRA. In the case of early retirement, a benefit is reduced by 5/9 of one percent for each month before normal retirement age, up to 36 months, or 6.67% per year. If the number of months exceeds 36, then the benefit is further reduced by 5/12 of one percent per month, or 5% per year[11].

Based on the calculations I just shared, I do not see any reason why anyone would take SS at FRA, which is a rather arbitrary number. If you are retired and are going to take benefits before age 70, why would you take them at FRA rather than 62? It costs you proportionally less the earlier you start taking your benefits.

I have heard many people say that they are retiring at FRA because that is when their SS will no longer be penalized. This statement frustrates me because some people view the FRA as if that is the age the government has decided you have the right to retire. Your FRA should not have anything to do with the decision to retire. It should be based on your health, family longevity, and financial fitness. Your age is most important when it comes to qualifying for Medicare. The government does not give retirement advice.

---

[11] https://www.ssa.gov/OACT/quickcalc/early_late.html

No matter what, you are taking a gamble on your lifespan when you take SS. If you think you may die prematurely, or if you doubt the SS system and want to ensure you get as much back as you can, you should start taking benefits at age 62.

For those who retire after age 62 and do not have significant net worth, it is likely best to initiate receipt of benefits whenever you retire to avoid putting too much pressure on your portfolio. If you are betting on living a long life and you can afford to wait, take benefits from age 70.

It is also worth considering the state of the stock market. If you are retired and drawing off your portfolio, it is more tempting to initiate government pension benefits if the stock market has recently decreased significantly, or if you are in the middle of a market correction. It is best to take portfolio distributions when the market is up so that you liquidate fewer shares to provide the cash you need. When markets are down, you must liquidate more shares, and a larger percentage of your portfolio, to provide the same income. Taking government pension benefits will help take pressure off your portfolio so it can recover from any previous losses.

In the case of spouses who have an age difference and a significant benefit difference, there are many complicating factors. In this example, Phil and Vivian remain married. Phil is older than Vivian but Vivian earned more money in her career and has the higher SS benefit. First, Phil has the smaller benefit but cannot receive his spousal benefit until Vivian also takes her benefit. At the same time, Vivian initiating receipt of her benefit before age 70 will result in a permanently lower benefit than she could have had if she had waited. There is a tradeoff in that you would not want to wait until Phil is past FRA because there is no increase in spousal benefits for waiting, but you also want to maximize Vivian's larger benefit.

Phil can take his own benefit until Vivian starts claiming benefits. The spousal benefit amount will automatically be added to Phil's benefit once Vivian begins receiving benefits. The main factors here are the age difference and the difference in benefits. Every situation is different, but you need to take this into consideration because your breakeven age could be different when considering spousal benefits.

You should not take SS if you are still working full time and have not yet reached FRA. If you take your benefits before full retirement age, the SSA will keep $1 for every $2 you earn above $23,400 (2025). They will keep $1 for every $3 you earn above $62,160 (2025). The penalty will apply until you reach full retirement age[12].

This rule is confusing, and I want to keep it simple: most people should not take their Social Security benefits until they are fully retired, need the income, or have reached age 70. If you have a shortened life expectancy or believe the Social Security program has a limited future, take your Social Security benefits from age 62 and get what you can while you can.

There is also a psychological component when it comes to this decision. Many people do not like spending a significant portion of their investments while they wait to take their government pensions. Even if they know they will have less money in the long term, they enjoy the safety of having their own funds and not depending on the government to support their lifestyle.

I would argue that SS is a benefit you have earned and should be viewed as a personal asset. The main difference is that the government controls the value of the asset. If it ever cuts benefit amounts or increases the payroll taxes that workers pay under the Federal Insurance Contributions Act (FICA)[13], it will effectively reduce the value of the asset.

---

[12] https://www.ssa.gov/faqs/en/questions/KA-01921.html

[13] https://www.ssa.gov/thirdparty/materials/pdfs/educators/What-is-FICA-Infographic-EN-05-10297.pdf

Employer pensions are viewed as personal assets and you usually have an opportunity to take a lump-sum payment rather than an annuity. In the U.S. you would roll your pension into an IRA or annuity, while in Canada it would likely roll into a Locked-in Retirement Account (LIRA) or Life Income Fund (LIF).

Your SS benefits are earned just like your employer pension benefits, but they are likely safer. In other words, had your FICA taxes gone into an account or annuity in your name, or if you could take SS benefits as a lump sum, they would be viewed as an asset, and the present value of SS payments through your expected lifetime should be viewed the same way when you are considering your net worth and future income.

There is the possibility that SS benefits could be legislatively reduced in the future, but I think the odds of that are low, especially for those already receiving benefits. I think it is more likely that there are changes to the full retirement age, maximum earnings limit ($176,100 in 2025), FICA tax rates (6.2% for SS and 1.45% for Medicare)[14], and spousal benefits in the future. Changes in those areas will be more tolerable for the public, and they are far less risky for politicians since SS recipients tend to vote at higher rates than younger voters.

Additionally, it is difficult for people who are already receiving benefits to adjust their lifestyle because of changes to benefit amounts. Those who are not yet receiving benefits can plan around any changes when deciding when to retire or initiate benefits. Some view this as a reason to initiate taking benefits as soon as possible. I think it is wise to watch for any legislative proposals seeking to reduce benefits. Consider initiating receipt of benefits if you feel any proposals that would affect you seem likely to pass.

As a result of changes to Social Security enacted in 1983, benefits are now

---

[14] https://www.irs.gov/taxtopics/tc751

expected to be payable in full on a timely basis until 2037, when the trust fund reserves are projected to become exhausted. At the point where the reserves are used up, continuing taxes are expected to be enough to pay 76 percent of scheduled benefits.[15] Thus, the Congress will need to make changes to the scheduled benefits and revenue sources for the program in the future. The Social Security Board of Trustees project that changes equivalent to an immediate reduction in benefits of about 13 percent, or an immediate increase in the combined payroll tax rate from 12.4 percent to 14.4 percent, or some combination of these changes, would be sufficient to allow full payment of the scheduled benefits for the next 75 years[16].

One of the reasons that the solvency of the SS Trust Fund is not better is because of low investment returns. The SS Trust Fund is invested entirely in U.S. Treasury securities[17]. Investing in this manner does nearly eliminate the possibility of investment loss, but it also ensures investment returns will be low when compared to the rest of the market[18].

---

[15] https://sgp.fas.org/crs/misc/RL33514.pdf

[16] https://www.ssa.gov/policy/docs/ssb/v70n3/v70n3p111.html

[17] https://www.cbpp.org/research/social-security/understanding-the-social-security-trust-funds-0#:~:text=The%20Social%20Security%20trust%20funds%20are%20invested%20entirely%20in%20U.S.,credit%20of%20the%20U.S.%20government

[18] https://home.treasury.gov/policy-issues/financing-the-government/interest-rate-statistics?data=yield

3

Canada Pension Plan (CPP) and Old Age Security (OAS)

Every time I hear a mean joke about being Canadian, I go to the hospital and get my feelings checked for free.

The Canada Pension Plan is like U.S. Social Security in that they both provide a retirement pension based on contributions you made while you were working. These contributions are made through payroll deductions or self-employment tax. The maximum monthly amount you can receive as a new CPP recipient starting to claim your pension at age 65 is $1,433.00 CAD (2025). The average monthly amount in January 2025 is $899.67 CAD[19].

Both systems also provide disability and death benefits. The CPP death benefit is a flat $2,500 CAD for each eligible participant ($255 USD for SS[20]). The survivor's benefit for those over 65 years of age is 60% of the value of their partner's pension, up to the maximum CPP benefit amount when combined with their own CPP benefit. If the surviving spouse is under 65, the survivor's pension is a fixed amount of $233.50 CAD (2025) plus 37.5% of the deceased spouse's pension. The maximum survivor's benefit in 2025 is $770.88 CAD per month[21] (($1,433.00 x 37.5%) + $233.50).

You must make at least $3,500 CAD before you begin making CPP contributions. This is referred to as the basic exemption amount. In 2025, the maximum pensionable earnings limit is $71,300 CAD[22]. Both the employer and employee make contributions of 5.95% (10.9% total) for income between $3,500 and $71,300. No contributions are made for income above this amount.

In contrast, the maximum U.S. SS earnings are $176,100 USD ($220,125 CAD). U.S. FICA tax rates are 6.2% for SS and 1.45% for Medicare (7.65% total). In the U.S., the employee and employer both contribute equally (15.3% combined),

---

[19] https://www.canada.ca/en/services/benefits/publicpensions/cpp/cpp-benefit/amount.html

[20] https://www.ssa.gov/survivor/amount

[21] https://www.savvynewcanadians.com/cpp-death-survivor-benefits/

[22] https://www.canada.ca/en/revenue-agency/services/tax/businesses/topics/payroll/payroll-deductions-contributions/canada-pension-plan-cpp/cpp-contribution-rates-maximums-exemptions.html

up to $176,100 USD[23]. Only the 1.45% Medicare tax is collected from each above that level.

You can take CPP as early as age 60 or as late as 70. Like SS, benefits are decreased if taken early and increased if taken late. Also, like SS, the bonus for taking benefits late is greater than the penalty for taking benefits early. In this case, your benefits will decrease by 0.6% per month (7.2% per year) if taken before 65 and increase by 0.7% per month (8.4% per year) if taken after your 65th birthday[24]. In comparison, the age at which you take your CPP benefits makes a slightly larger difference to your benefit amount than it does for SS.

The Old Age Security program is the Canadian government's largest pension program. It is funded out of general tax revenues. This means that you do not pay into the program directly. SS is funded through FICA taxes and you make CPP contributions, but there is no separate tax for OAS. The OAS program also includes the Guaranteed Income Supplement and Allowance amounts, which I am not going to discuss. An Allowance for the Survivor is also available, but only for surviving spouses between the ages of 60 and 64[25].

The maximum OAS benefit for Quarter 1 of 2025 is $727.67 at age 65. Those over 75 can receive up to $800.44. To receive the maximum benefit, you need to live in Canada for at least 40 years after the age of 18. There is a minimum residency requirement of 10 years before you become eligible for any OAS benefits[26]. If you do not meet the full 40 years, you will receive a prorated benefit based on how many years you have lived in Canada as an adult.

---

[23] https://www.ssa.gov/benefits/retirement/planner/maxtax.html

[24] https://www.canada.ca/en/services/benefits/publicpensions/cpp/cpp-benefit/when-start.html

[25] https://www.canada.ca/en/services/benefits/publicpensions/old-age-security/payments.html

[26] https://www.canada.ca/en/services/benefits/publicpensions/old-age-security/benefit-amount.html

The formula is:

(X/40) x Maximum OAS Benefit

Fortunately, your ratio will continue to go up even after initiating receipt of your OAS benefit, if you live in Canada. For example, if you move from Canada to the U.S. at age 28, you will have 10 years of OAS residence history. When you move from the U.S. back to Canada, your ratio will continue to go up each year you live in Canada until your 70th birthday.

Unlike CPP, OAS benefits are not available until full retirement age, or 65 in Canada. Your benefit will increase if you delay receipt, as with CPP but at a lower rate. OAS benefits increase by 0.6% per month of delay (7.2% annually), for a maximum increase of 36% if receipt is delayed until age 70[27]. When comparing OAS with SS and CPP, it is least beneficial to delay OAS benefits, and most beneficial to delay CPP benefits. Conversely, the penalty for taking CPP early is greater than that for SS.

Pension	FRA	Earliest	Penalty	Latest	Increase
SS	67	62	6.00%	70	8.00%
CPP	65	60	7.20%	70	8.40%
OAS	65	65		70	7.20%

I view the FRA as an arbitrary number that should be ignored. The percentage increase or decrease for delaying taking benefits changes slightly at FRA, but it is really a sliding scale. Do not base your decision on when to take benefits

---

[27] https://www.moneysense.ca/columns/retired-money/delaying-cpp-and-oas-to-age-70/

on "full" benefits being available at age 65. The maximum benefit is available at 70. The cash-flow breakeven analysis can be done the same way as was shown for SS.

According to Statistics Canada, the life expectancy for men in 2018 is 79.9. Female life expectancy is 84.1[28]. Early deaths due to accidents, illness, and a variety of other causes bring that average down. This is why life expectancy tables increase with age. Every year you live reduces your chances of premature death from unnatural causes.

It is interesting to note that female life expectancy is consistently higher than male life expectancy across the globe. The odds of premature death are low when only considering yourself. When considering a married couple, the odds of one partner passing prematurely doubles. For that reason, many couples want to "hedge their bet" when it comes to government pensions. Even though they know they will get more in the long term if they both wait to take benefits at age 70, they also want to make sure they get something from their government pensions.

If both spouses are the same age and expect similar benefit amounts, you may decide to take one spouse's benefits early and the other at 70. This way you ensure you get some benefits from one spouse while maximizing the other spouse's benefits. The problem with this approach is it can be detrimental if the wrong spouse dies prematurely.

Other things that should be taken into consideration if you will be taking some government benefits early and some late are:

- How old is each spouse?
- Does one spouse have a larger benefit than the other?
- Who owns their other assets (retirement accounts, pension, rental

---

[28] https://www150.statcan.gc.ca/t1/tbl1/en/tv.action?pid=1310011401

property, etc.)?
· Which country are you a tax resident of?
· Which benefits should you take early if you qualify for OAS, CPP and SS?

In Canada, everyone files their own tax return. Tax planning is usually done jointly for married couples filing jointly in the U.S. Tax planning is done both jointly and individually in Canada. It is done jointly through your savings patterns, pension sharing, and the income splitting election on your tax returns. It is done individually when you are deciding on annual retirement account distribution amounts.

If you only qualify for OAS and CPP (not SS), you likely want to take OAS early as it is the smaller benefit. If you believe you have a shortened life expectancy but want to hedge your bets in case you live longer, then you may want to take CPP first as it is likely the larger benefit, and you can begin CPP at age 60 but OAS payments cannot begin until 65. Your smaller OAS benefit can continue to grow and provide additional income after age 70.

You may wonder if it makes sense to take benefits early to preserve investment capital, pay for vacations or start gifting to children. There are four reasons it makes sense to take government pensions before age 70:

· You need the money
· You have a shortened life expectancy
· To preserve investment capital
· To ensure you get what you can from your pensions if you are worried about the plan's solvency.

4

U.S. Retirement Savings

Retirement is like a long vacation in Las Vegas. The goal is to enjoy it to the fullest, but not so fully that you run out of money.

– Jonathan Clements

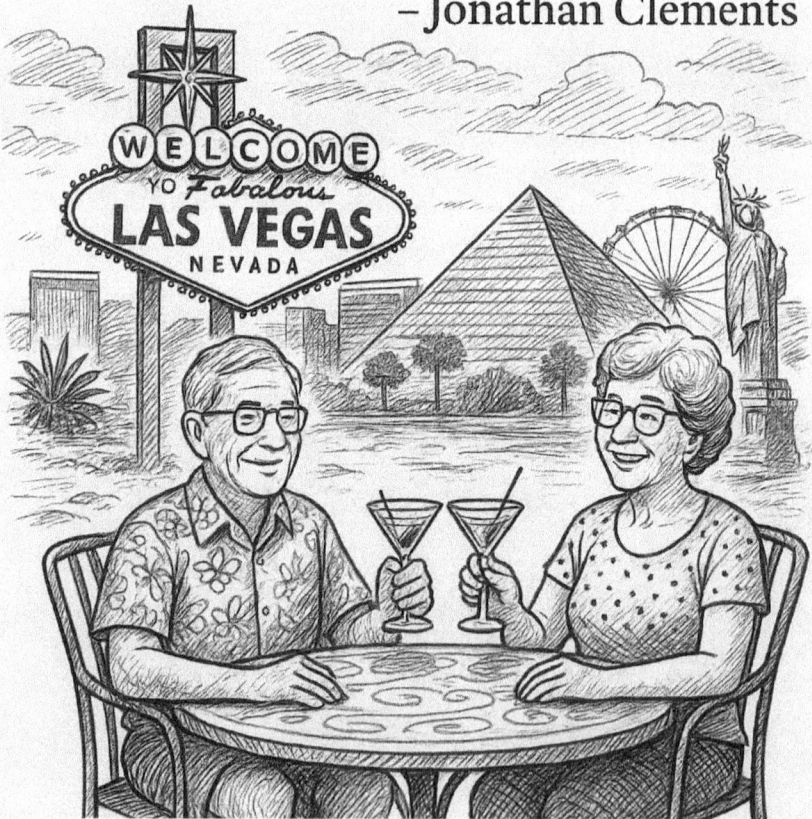

There are many types of retirement savings vehicles that can be used to defer income, and the payment of tax, in the U.S. while you are working. Employers may offer a 401(k), 403(b), defined benefit (DB) pension plan, 457 or other employer-sponsored retirement plan. Self-employed people may be saving in a Simplified Employee Pension (SEP) Individual Retirement Account (IRA), Savings Incentive Match Plan for Employees (SIMPLE) IRA, Solo 401(k), or their own DB pension plan. People usually transfer their employer-sponsored plan to a Rollover IRA once they retire.

All taxpayers are eligible to contribute to an IRA if they, or their spouse, do not have an employer-sponsored retirement plan, regardless of their income level. Your ability to contribute to an IRA may be limited if your income is too high and if you or your spouse have an employer-sponsored plan available at work. If your spouse is covered by an employer-sponsored retirement plan, IRA deductibility phases out between $218,000 and $228,000 for married couples in 2023[29]. If you are covered by an employer-sponsored retirement plan, IRA deductibility phases out between $116,000 and $136,000 for joint filers[30].

---

[29] https://www.irs.gov/retirement-plans/2023-ira-deduction-limits-effect-of-modified-agi
-on-deduction-if-you-are-not-covered-by-a-retirement-plan-at-work

[30] https://www.irs.gov/retirement-plans/2023-ira-deduction-limits-effect-of-modified-agi
-on-deduction-if-you-are-covered-by-a-retirement-plan-at-work

If you are covered by a retirement plan at work, use this table to determine if your modified AGI attects the amount of your deduction.		
If your filing status is...	**And your modified AGI is...**	**Then you can take...**
single or head of household	**$73,000 or less**	a full deduction up to the amount of your contribution limit.
single or head of household	more than $78,000 but less than $82,000	a partial deduction.
single or head of household	$83,000 or more	no deduction.
married filing jointly or qualifying widow(er)	**$116,000 or less**	a full deduction up to the amount of your contribution limit.
married filing jointly or qualifying widow(er)	more than $116,000 but less than $136,000	a partial deduction.
married filing jointly or qualifying widow(er)	$136,000 or more	no deduction.
married filing separately	less than $10,000	a partial deduction.
married filing separately	$10,000 or more	no deduction.
If you file separately and did not live with your spouse at any time during the year, your IRA deduction is determined under the "Single" filing status.		

IRA distributions after age 59½ are fully taxable as ordinary income for U.S. citizens, Green Card holders and U.S. tax residents. Distributions prior to 59½ also incur a 10% early withdrawal penalty tax. IRA distributions must now begin by April 1st in the year after you turn 73, for those who have not yet begun Required Minimum Distributions (RMDs). Under the old rules (prior to 2020), you could not make any IRA contributions after you reached the RMD age of 70½.

The Setting Every Community Up for Retirement Enhancement (SECURE) Act removed that restriction, and you can now make IRA contributions for as long as you have earned income[31]. IRA RMDs are still required by April 1st in the year after you turn 73, even if you are still contributing. RMDs from employer-sponsored retirement plans can now be delayed until April 1st of the year after

---

[31] https://www.irs.gov/retirement-plans/retirement-plan-and-ira-required-minimum-distributions-faqs

you retire[32].

The SECURE Act brought other changes in 2020. Most notably, it limited the "stretch" provision previously available to Inherited IRA beneficiaries. The "stretch" term refers to the ability of Inherited IRA owners to take RMDs based on their own life expectancy rather than that of the previous owner, who was often much older. By stretching the timeframe over which a beneficiary can take distributions, you reduce their taxable income each year over that period. Reducing their taxable income may result in them paying lower tax rates, reducing their tax liability each year and over the life of the IRA.

For IRA owners who passed away prior to 2020 and had not yet begun RMDs, their beneficiaries were able to take the RMDs according to their own life expectancy table. In tax years 2020 and later, most non-spouse IRA beneficiaries must take their Inherited IRA distributions over a maximum period of 10 years[33]. This is a big change considering that IRA beneficiaries can be any age, dramatically increasing the amount of IRA income younger beneficiaries must take each year. This can drastically increase the amount that is paid in tax.

If the beneficiary is a non-human, such as a trust or charity, the IRA must be fully distributed by the end of the fifth year after the death of the owner. The Internal Revenue Service (IRS) has clarified its guidance for RMDs for Inherited IRA owners. The RMD tables should be used to determine annual RMD amounts, and the balance must be distributed in full within either five or 10 years, depending on whether the IRA beneficiary is a human or not.

For example, a 45-year-old inherits a $1 million IRA in 2019 from a parent who had not yet started RMDs. A 45-year-old has a single life expectancy

---

[32] https://www.fidelity.com/learning-center/personal-finance/retirement/options-taking-first-rmd

[33] https://www.fidelity.com/retirement-ira/inherited-ira-rmd

of 38.8[34]. This means they must distribute $25,773 or 2.58% (1/38.8) in the year after death. The single life expectancy will go down by one each year, so their distribution factor in the second year would be 37.8 or 2.65%. If the IRA had appreciated back to the original value of $1 million, this would result in a second-year RMD of $26,455. The distribution factor will decrease by one each year, so the distributions will get bigger and bigger until they are large enough to cause the account value to decrease annually. These distributions could be spread over 30 years or more.

Compare this to the new rules under the SECURE Act and our 45-year-old beneficiary has a few options. They can take only the RMD for nine years and the balance in year 10, equal distributions of approximately 10% of the account value each year, the entire balance as a lump sum in any year, or any combination of distributions within the first 10 years, as long as the RMD is taken annually.

Depending on the income of the beneficiary, a $26,455 distribution may not push them into the next tax bracket. A distribution of $100,000+ will likely push them into the next tax bracket. Taking a lump-sum distribution of over $1 million will result in them paying the highest federal tax rate of 37% on much of that distribution (50%+ if living in Canada).

When it comes to the timing of when to take distributions, conventional wisdom says that you should defer the payment of taxes for as long as possible. For people who have taxable savings and investments, Roth IRAs and Traditional IRAs, this will result in distributing the taxable accounts first (to get rid of the continual investment income), Roth IRAs second (tax-free), and Traditional IRAs last (fully taxable).

A "Roth conversion" is when a person "rolls" or distributes funds from their Traditional IRA into their Roth IRA. Tax must be paid on the IRA distribution,

---

[34] https://www.irs.gov/publications/p590b

but the IRS tax code allows for a matching Roth IRA contribution in the same year. Roth IRA distributions are tax-free after age 59½. If Roth IRA distributions are taken before then, contributions come out tax-free but there is a 10% penalty on earnings.

Roth IRAs also have the added benefits of no RMDs for the original owner, and tax-free income for that owner's heirs after their death. RMDs must be taken from Inherited Roth IRAs in the same manner as with Traditional IRAs. Roth conversions cannot be done with RMD distributions.

When a person retires prior to age 70, eliminating most of their taxable income, they are faced with deciding what they will use for living expenses until they are forced to start taking SS. This planning is most effective when a person has a Roth IRA, personal savings, taxable investments, and qualified investment accounts (401(k), IRA). The goal is to take money out of the IRA during your early retirement years while your income is low and before you are forced to take more income in the form of RMDs, minimum Registered Retirement Income Fund (RRIF) distributions, SS, CPP, and OAS benefits. Generally, this must be done between retirement and age 70, because that is when you must initiate government pension benefits.

Only those who have large IRAs or other qualified account balances should consider Roth conversions. The idea is to take advantage of lower tax rates now before you are forced into higher tax brackets in the future. If your IRA RMDs are not going to be large enough to force you into a higher tax bracket, you are better off deferring the payment of tax for as long as possible.

The U.S. tax brackets are:

Tax rate	Single filer	Married filing jointly (or surviving spouse)	Head of household	Married filing separately
10%	$0 to $11,925	$0 to $23,850	$0 to $17,000	$0 to $11,925
12%	$11,926 to $48,475	$23,851 to $96,950	$17,001 to $64,850	$11,926 to $48,475
22%	$48,476 to $103,350	$96,951 to $206,700	$64,851 to $103,350	$48,476 to $103,350
24%	$103,351 to $197,300	$206,701 to $394,600	$103,351 to $197,300	$103,351 to $197,300
32%	$197,301 to $250,525	$394,601 to $501,050	$197,301 to $250,500	$197,301 to $250,525
35%	$250,526 to $626,350	$501,051 to $751,600	$250,501 to $626,350	$250,526 to $375,800
37%	$626,351 or more	$751,601 or more	$626,351 or more	$375,801 or more

There are a few considerations one should keep in mind when deciding when to take income:

- Defer the payment of tax for as long as possible, all else being equal;
- Only take more income than you need for living expenses if it will result in paying a lower tax rate over time;
- If your investments are greater than you will need for your lifetime, take a generational perspective by considering things like your heirs' tax situation, gifting, and charitable giving;
- The "OAS clawback" if you are a Canadian resident;
- Medicare Part B premiums if you will be living in or spending significant time in the U.S.;
- Affordable Care Act subsidies until age 65;
- The Alternative Minimum Tax (AMT);
- The Net Investment Income Tax (NIIT);
- The Medicare Surtax;
- State income taxes;
- Other government benefits you may be receiving;
- Student aid and student loan applications for your children and dependent grandchildren.

Your lifetime cash flows should be mapped out to plan this properly. It is common for those who live a long life to be pushed into higher tax brackets in their later years as their life expectancy gets smaller and their RMDs get larger. If you know your RMDs will not push you into higher tax brackets until your late 80s, you may or may not want to do Roth conversions depending on your personal life expectancy.

At the end of the day, all these decisions are a gamble based on how long you live. You could plan perfectly if you knew how long you would live. If I know you are going to die at age 72, I will recommend you take all your government pensions at age 62, forget about taxes and enjoy your money. If I know you are going to live to be 100, I will recommend you take all your government pensions at age 70, and do Roth conversions as much as possible before then so you can pay consistent tax rates throughout your lifetime.

The Rule of 72 is a simple way to determine how long an investment will take to double given a fixed annual rate of return. By dividing 72 by the annual rate of return, investors obtain an estimate of how many years it will take for the initial investment to double in size[35]. Most younger investors require a long-term annual rate of return of at least 5% to 6%. The Rule of 72 indicates that an investment returning 6% will double in 12 years.

$100 returning 6% annually will grow to $240 in 15 years. After paying 22% in tax, the value will be $187. In contrast, if an investor pays 12% tax at the beginning of the period through a Roth conversion, the starting value will be $88. After 15 years with a 6% return, the ending value will be $211, with no tax to pay. Not all the tax would be paid at the same time at the end of the 15 years, but I am trying to keep this simple. Only do Roth conversions if you are expecting a significantly higher tax rate in the future.

Generally, I recommend Roth conversions to clients if they will be able to stay out of the 22% tax bracket, or the 32% tax bracket. It is not worth it if going from 24% to 22%, or from 37% or 35% to the 32% bracket.

The amount of time until you are forced to take RMD income should be one of the primary considerations. For example, if your RMDs start next year,

---

[35] https://www.investopedia.com/terms/r/ruleof72.asp

but you can take some funds out this year and save 2%, I recommend you do that. If you are 62 and will not have to take RMDs for another 13 years, the difference in tax rate is going to have to be larger.

Another important consideration, particularly when you come to estate planning, is the tax bracket of your heirs. For example, if you are living in Florida and you have one child who is an attorney in Ontario, you are likely paying 12%, 22% or 24% on your IRA distributions, while your child is paying 53.53% on all income. In this case, Roth conversions should be considered for your child's benefit.

Roth conversions should not be done by those who are tax residents of Canada. Making Roth IRA contributions, even if through a Roth conversion, will taint your Roth IRA and cause all future investment income on those Canadian contributions to be taxable, which defeats the purpose. Canadian residents are already exposed to the more compressed Canadian tax brackets. Since all IRA distributions are fully taxable in Canada, it is unlikely a Roth conversion would make sense even if you did not have to worry about the Roth being tainted[36].

The factors to consider for Roth conversions are:

1. How old are you when you retire?
2. What is your retirement income without government pensions or retirement account distributions?
3. What will your income be after RMDs and government pensions begin?
4. What is the difference in tax brackets before and after RMDs and government pensions begin?
5. What tax brackets are you projected to be in for the remainder of your life? Your distribution planning should be coordinated with your retirement

---

[36] https://expattaxprofessionals.com/blog/article/roth-ira-taxation-for-expats-in-canada#:
~:text=The%20treaty%20provides%20that%20if,such%20time%20will%20be%20subject

projections.

6. How much remaining room do you have in the lower tax brackets?
7. Do you have other funds to sustain your lifestyle?
8. What is the projected tax bracket of your heirs?

Another underutilized retirement savings vehicle is the Health Savings Account (HSA)[37]. The HSA is the most advantageous account available to save for retirement. Contributions are an above-the-line deduction, like IRA or 401(k) contributions. This is especially beneficial for high-income earners because there are no income limits for HSA contributions, and for those that use the standard deduction. Investments grow tax-free and, as with a Roth IRA, distributions used to pay for qualified medical expenses are tax-free. This is also true for people who retire in Canada as there are no rules around where the medical expenses must occur geographically.

The only requirement to contribute to an HSA is you must be enrolled in a High-Deductible Health Plan (HDHP). For 2025, the IRS defines an HDHP as any plan with a deductible of at least $1,650 for an individual or $3,300 for a family. A HDHP's total yearly out-of-pocket expenses (including deductibles, copayments, and coinsurance) cannot be more than $8,300 for an individual or $16,600 for a family[38]. This limit does not apply to out-of-network services.

The HSA is the best retirement savings vehicle because:

1. It is the only account available in the U.S. which allows for deductible contributions, tax-free growth, and tax-free distributions.
2. Anyone with an HDHP can qualify, with no income limitations.
3. It allows above-the-line deductions.
4. Like an IRA, there is no penalty for distributions after the age of 65, even if not used for qualifying medical expenses. Distributions taken prior to

---

[37] https://www.irs.gov/pub/irs-drop/n-04-2.pdf

[38] https://www.forbes.com/advisor/health-insurance/high-deductible-health-plan/

age 65 and not used for qualifying medical expenses, are fully taxable and subject to a 20% penalty[39].

HSAs are not included in the Canada-U.S. Tax Treaty[40] (the Treaty) so growth within the account is not tax-free for Canadian residents. The funds within the account should be invested in coordination with the rest of your portfolio. Once you move to Canada, the account should be invested so that the income generated is primarily capital gains. Capital gains are preferable because the income can be deferred until the security is sold, and capital gains receive preferential tax treatment on both sides of the border.

Another important thing to note is that tracking investment income in an HSA can be difficult, especially from a Canadian perspective. Individuals moving from Canada to certain U.S. states have a similar challenge with the income generated in their registered retirement accounts in Canada. Some states do not honor the Treaty[41], so Canadian registered accounts are not recognized and are taxed just like brokerage accounts at the state level.

There are two reasons tracking income in HSAs and RRSPs is difficult:

- The custodians do not track the income because it is the distribution that is potentially taxable in their home country, not the investment income.
- Currency conversion must be made on the date of each transaction.

For example, HSAs are U.S. accounts and will have to be kept on a U.S. custodial platform. Hence, they will only be able to use U.S. securities. Finding a custodian to hold your HSA as a Canadian resident will be difficult. The most likely result will be the bank where the account is held will freeze the account

---

[39] https://smartasset.com/insurance/hsa-withdrawal-rules

[40] https://www.irs.gov/businesses/international-businesses/canada-tax-treaty-documents

[41] https://ustaxesblog.wordpress.com/2017/07/21/does-states-conform-to-the-federal-tax-treaties/

for trading purposes once a Canadian address is listed on the account. You will only be able to sell securities in the account after it is frozen.

A worst-case scenario is if the bank or custodian liquidates the account after you leave the U.S. and mails you a cheque. You should check with your bank or custodian before leaving the U.S. if you plan on moving out of the country. For this reason, it is likely best if you purchase a security that will be good to hold long term before entering Canada. An example may be a growth stock fund. If you do this, your Canadian basis in the account will be the value on the day you enter the country.

If you hold the fund long term, income will only be generated from dividends and capital gains. The gains will be based on the exchange rate on the day you entered the country, and the exchange rate on the day shares are sold. If used for qualified medical expenses, no additional tax will be due. If not, the entire distribution will be subject to taxes in the U.S., plus the 20% penalty if you are under 65.

Only half of capital gains are taxable in Canada, making HSAs an extremely efficient retirement savings vehicle, especially if used for qualified medical expenses. Unfortunately, many banks and custodians do not allow stock investments in these accounts; rather, they are interest-bearing accounts.

Upon the death of the HSA account owner, the spouse can assume ownership of the HSA as their own. Once the surviving spouse passes away, the HSA is fully taxable to all non-spouse beneficiaries in the year of death. Interestingly, the HSA is taxable to the beneficiary, not on the deceased owner's last tax return, and there are no stretch provisions available. If you retire before you are eligible for Medicare at age 65, HSA funds can be used to pay for Consolidated Omnibus Budget Reconciliation Act (COBRA) premiums for continued health coverage, but not private insurance[42].

Many Americans are going to retire with money in an employer- sponsored retirement plan, an IRA, a Roth IRA, taxable investments, a HSA, and savings and chequing accounts. Those who have worked in Canada will likely also have an RRSP, some taxable savings in Canadian dollars, and possibly a pension or LIRA. Everyone who has worked in either country will also have government pensions to support their retirement lifestyle.

When you consider the different currencies involved, many people will have 11 or more accounts or sources of income. Multiply that by two for a married couple. So how do you decide which pensions and accounts to draw income from and in what order? I will start with U.S. income sources for those living in the U.S.

If we picture the stereotypical 65-year-old couple who are both healthy and retire to Florida, where there is no state income tax, conventional wisdom tells us to delay SS until age 70 to get the maximum benefit and delay the payment of tax for as long as possible by living off taxable savings and Roth IRAs until RMDs are required. If your IRAs are large enough that your RMDs will push you into higher tax brackets later in life, you should consider doing some Roth conversions until you reach age 70 and are taking SS.

In the real world, normal doesn't exist. Every person is different, and each family is unique. Every detail should be considered when planning for retirement income. Some couples have age differences, while some keep their finances separate, have health issues, are supporting adult children or grandchildren, have marital and family issues, have unconventional families, or deal with disabilities, etc. For this example, we will use a couple who retires in Florida. Jim is 64 and Pam is 57. Jim has an FRA of 66 and four months;

---

[42] https://www.dol.gov/agencies/ebsa/about-ebsa/our-activities/resource-center/publications/an-employees-guide-to-health-benefits-under-cobra

Pam's is 67.

When they retire, they both consolidate their 401(k) and 403(b) into IRAs ($2 million total). They also have taxable savings of $400,000, hold a $50,000 HSA, and qualify for SS. Pam is a teacher and stayed home to raise the children for several years. Her SS benefit is much smaller than Jim's. She is healthy and both her parents lived into their 90s. Jim is an engineer who retired in management at a large corporation. He has high blood pressure, high cholesterol and has already had one bout with cancer. His father died in his 50s from a heart attack, his mother died in her 60s from cancer, and his older sister died a few years ago at 71 from a heart attack.

Jim would maximize his SS benefit by waiting until age 70, but due to Jim's health issues and lack of family longevity, he should take his SS as soon as he retires at age 65. It is reasonable to believe he may not make it to his 80s, so it is best to get what he can from SS now. The worst-case scenario for him is if he lives into his 80s and gets less from SS than he would have if he had delayed. Conversely, if he waits and passes away in the next 15 years, he will receive less gross lifetime benefits.

Jim must take his SS before Pam can take her spousal benefit, but she does not have to start her benefit just because he is taking his. In this case, it is likely she will live well into her 80s, so she should wait and take her spousal benefit at age 67. It is likely she will get an SS survivor's benefit someday when Jim is gone. Her survivor's benefit will be equivalent to Jim's FRA benefit, even if Jim receives a reduced benefit for taking benefits early. Having Jim take his SS benefits early will hinder their ability to do Roth conversions in the years before he turns 72. They should still attempt to do some Roth conversions but must also keep in mind that Pam is seven years younger and will be able to take distributions over her own life expectancy should Jim pass away.

The two big jumps in tax rate in the U.S. are from 12% to 22% and from 24% to 32%. When doing Roth conversions, I generally recommend clients max out either the 12% bracket or the 24% bracket. In theory, if you are going to max out the 22% bracket, you may as well max out the 24% bracket as well. Likewise, if you are going to max out the 10% bracket, you may as well max out the 12% bracket. The exception to this is if you have significant capital gains income. You want to stay in the 10% bracket, because capital gains are taxed at 0% for those in the 10% bracket.

For those who have large IRAs, it is likely your RMDs will push you into the 22% bracket or higher when combined with your other income. Those people should max out the 12% bracket with Roth conversions until age 73. For those with smaller IRAs, you are likely going to fall in the 10% or 12% bracket no matter what you do, so you should delay the payment of tax for as long as possible and no Roth conversions should be done. For people on the cusp, you should try to remain in the 12% bracket for as long as possible by supplementing your IRA distributions with funds from a Roth IRA or taxable savings account. Once you reach age 73 and are receiving SS and RMDs, the only tax planning to be done is generational.

Pensions create some unique considerations. The most common type of pension is an employer- sponsored defined benefit plan. The employer usually makes all the contributions. These can be sponsored by employers, unions, trade groups, municipalities, states, or the federal government. The final benefit is usually based on a formula that includes factors such as retirement age, age at which benefits commence, number of years worked with the organization, and average income or income over the last five years prior to retirement. Employees often have the option of either taking their lifetime pension or rolling a lump sum, based on the commuted value of future cash flows, into an IRA.

I usually recommend rolling the commuted value into your IRA for a few reasons:

1. The assumed return on investment is usually low for pension benefits.

History suggests you should do better in a well-balanced portfolio.

2. A well-balanced portfolio will produce more lifetime income than the pension benefits in most cases. The caveat is that we do not know what returns markets will produce in the future, so we cannot guarantee future returns will be like past returns. That said, when projecting rates of return for financial planning purposes, I use rates that are conservative and based on historical averages.

3. Pensions are not usually an asset you leave to your heirs. Many pensions offer different distribution options. These usually include "single life", "period certain" and different degrees of "joint life" or "second to die" options. Single life means the pension is paid over the life of the pensioner only. Period certain means the pension is paid for life, or for a minimum period, typically 10 years, whichever is greater. If the pensioner passes away before that period is over, the pension will continue to be paid to the beneficiary or estate. With joint life and second to die options, the pension continues to be paid to the surviving spouse. The spouse's survivor benefit could be anywhere from 25% to 100% of the pensioner's original benefit. These distribution options are nice while you are alive, but the pension will end with the death of your spouse. There will be no asset to pass to your children or grandchildren unless you choose a period certain distribution option. That said, if all the pension benefits are not needed for living expenses, the remainder can be saved for future generations or used to purchase life insurance for their benefit.

4. Your pension benefits are not your asset. They are technically a liability of the company you worked for, and any money set aside for pension benefit payments is the company's asset. This is important because your pension benefits are exposed to the risk that the business may not be able to satisfy your pension liability when the time comes. All pensions, both public and private, are at risk of benefits being reduced or eliminated during bankruptcy proceedings, buyouts, or mergers. There

are examples of this in the private[43] and public sector[44].

Once you take your lump-sum pension benefit and roll it into your IRA, it is yours. Your employer's finances no longer have any impact on your own. Many people view receiving pension benefits as safer than taking the lump sum and exposing it to the risk of the stock market, because they feel their pension benefits are "guaranteed". However, nothing is guaranteed until it is in your hand. Yes, there are risks associated with investing in stocks. If you are risk averse, your exposure to the stock market should be limited, and you should invest primarily in fixed income securities.

Another option is purchasing an annuity, which may provide more lifetime income than the pension. As with the pension, your annuity benefits are only guaranteed by the insurance company that pays them, and that insurance company may go bankrupt. Investing on your own gives you the ability to determine your own risk tolerance. Your investments will be exposed to thousands of companies if you invest in mutual funds and exchange traded funds (ETFs). This means your risk will be spread out over thousands of companies. Pension and annuity benefits are dependent on the health of the payer, and the investments they hold. Pension and annuity benefits present more concentrated risk.

One of the goals of a well-diversified portfolio is to prevent deterioration of purchasing power by providing a rate of return that is greater than inflation. Many pensions do not provide an annual cost-of-living adjustment, and many pensions that are indexed do not keep up with inflation. This could result in the loss of purchasing power over time. Your budget will get tighter because of inflation, but your benefit will remain the same or increase at a slower rate.

---

[43] https://www.visualcapitalist.com/the-20-biggest-bankruptcies-in-u-s-history/

[44] https://www.pewtrusts.org/en/research-and-analysis/articles/2020/07/07/by-the-numbe rs-a-look-at-municipal-bankruptcies-over-the-past-20-years

There is the possibility that pension benefits could be reduced in the future. The SS Trust Fund is expected to be depleted between 2033-2037[45], and some studies project that this will happen sooner[46]. If it does happen, estimates show that current revenues to SS through payroll taxes will cover approximately 77% of current projected benefits. This will result in SS benefits being reduced by about 23%[47]. Government projections tend to be too rosy, so I would expect that reduction to be even greater unless legislation is passed to provide additional funding to SS. The COVID-19 pandemic has also hurt SS solvency[48]. This is primarily due to increased unemployment, decreased payroll tax revenues, and people initiating receipt of benefits due to being laid off or retiring early.

Municipalities and corporations can also file for bankruptcy, seeking relief from the unfunded liability portion of their pension plan. That is unthinkable to many people, but it has happened in the past. There have been situations where municipalities have issued bonds and then invested the proceeds in stocks to try and make up the difference on their pension liabilities. That is like going to the casino to win back what you have already lost. Of course, this is very risky and only exacerbates the problem. Part of the reason many pensions are underfunded is because investment performance was lower than projected.

At the end of the day, your pension is only as safe as the entity promising it. Many pensioners have faith in their former employers, but most companies have a lifespan, and financial mismanagement by government entities is nothing new. Pensions are great for those who cannot risk that income, but it

---

[45] https://www.forbes.com/sites/stevevernon/2024/03/21/will-social-security-run-out-of-money-if-so-when/

[46] https://www.aarp.org/social-security/benefits-trust-fund-runs-out-by-2031/?msockid=26345d234a1d6aec072f49904b996bcc

[47] https://www.ssa.gov/oact/TR/2023/

[48] https://www.forbes.com/sites/bobcarlson/2020/04/22/the-pandemic-reduces-social-securitys-solvency/?sh=55aa8b3dff31

is also like investing much of your net worth in one bond. You are subject to the same business risk and your return on investment is relatively low.

The pension is also a liability to the issuer. Only the federal government can print money, which means businesses and municipalities may not be able to meet their obligations if their finances are not managed properly. Some senators argue that even states should be able to declare bankruptcy[49]. Several municipalities have declared bankruptcy in the past. Some of the larger ones are Detroit (MI), Stockton (CA) and San Bernadino (CA).

People who are self-employed have the option of starting a defined benefit plan for their company. DB plans are no longer popular with large employers because they are too expensive to fund. DB plans should be considered as a retirement planning option for those who are self-employed or independent contractors, and companies that have few employees but high profits. DB plans give self-employed people the opportunity to defer significantly more income than a 401(k), SEP IRA or SIMPLE IRA.

Rather than limiting contributions to a dollar amount like a 401(k) ($19,500 in 2020), DB plans limit contributions to a percentage of income (25%), and by the projected benefit the contributions will produce in retirement (maximum $280,000 in 2025). Higher income and a shorter contribution period will result in the ability to make larger contributions. These plans will be most attractive for those who are nearing retirement, have income of $200,000 or more, and have significant disposable income available for saving.

Once those with individual DB plans retire, they usually roll the DB plan balance into an IRA. This is the best thing to do as their company will likely be dissolved after retirement. Once the funds are in the IRA, it can be managed with the rest of their portfolio. I have seen this used most with those who go

---

[49] https://thehill.com/homenews/campaign/495169-state-bankruptcy-furor-shakes-up-mc connell-reelection-bid/

into private consulting later in their career.

For those who have employer-sponsored DB plans and limited other assets, it may be best to either leave the pension in place or take the commuted value and purchase an annuity. When your pension is your only financial asset and you have a "guarantee" from your previous employer or an insurance company, you want that asset to be as safe as possible. Pensions and annuities are typically paid for life, whereas you can run out of money if you roll the lump sum into an IRA and have a long lifespan.

For those who have a DB plan and other financial assets, rolling your pension benefits into an IRA can allow you to do tax planning that would otherwise not be possible. Many pensions require receipt of benefits to begin at a specific age or within a specified number of years after retirement. This can limit your ability to do Roth conversions.

Earlier I recommended that you should wait until age 70 to take SS benefits if you can afford to. That is partly to receive larger benefits and partly to allow more flexibility in tax planning between retirement and age 70. The same principle applies here. You want to take advantage of low-income years and use the opportunity to move money into a Roth IRA, so it is never taxed again.

You want to defer income and tax for as long as possible unless you have an opportunity to pay the tax at a lower rate sooner. Taking pension benefits before you must limits your ability to do this. Rolling your pension into an IRA will allow you to defer that income until age 73 if you choose. A qualified tax advisor should help determine the proper amount of Roth conversion each year.

From an investment perspective, some advisors believe pensions should be viewed as a bond proxy. They argue that current bond yields should be used to determine the present value of pensions benefit payments. This present value should be viewed as part of the fixed income portion of your portfolio. For example, you may have a present value of pension benefits of $500,000, and $1 million in other investment assets. If your portfolio allocation calls for 60% equity and 40% fixed income, this theory says you should have $900,000 in equity and $600,000 in fixed income. Since the present value of your pension is $500,000, only $100,000 of your investment assets will be invested in fixed income.

You could also make the same argument that the present value of SS, CPP and OAS benefits should be considered part of the fixed income portion of your portfolio. If the present value for SS, CPP and OAS are included in this example, 100% of the $1 million in investable assets will be in equities. I do not agree with this logic because it is too risky. In this situation, I would recommend that $600,000 be invested in equity and $400,000 be invested in fixed income regardless of the potential pension benefits.

For those with significant assets and charitable intentions, IRAs provide an opportunity not available with other accounts. After reaching age 70½, you can make qualified charitable distributions (QCDs) of up to $108,000 per year directly from your IRA[50]. By paying directly from your IRA, you never pay tax on the distribution. The charity will not have to pay tax on it either, so the government is cut out completely and more funds are available for the charity to do its work.

Effective from tax year 2020 onwards, the QCD limit per tax year will be reduced by the aggregate amount of deductions allowed for prior tax years, due to the changes brought about by the SECURE Act. This means deductible IRA contributions made for the year you reach age 70½ and later years can reduce your annual QCD allowance[51]. You must be working and have earned

---

[50] https://www.schwab.com/learn/story/reducing-rmds-with-qcds?msockid=26345d234a1d6aec072f49904b996bcc

[51] https://www.kitces.com/blog/secure-act-qualified-charitable-distributions-qcd-ira-contribution-age-repeal-70-1-2-anti-abuse-reduction/

income to be eligible to make IRA contributions. The SECURE Act removed the age limit for IRA contributions.

5

Canada Retirement Savings

You can't buy happiness, but you can live in **Canada.** And that's pretty much the same thing.

The retirement savings system in Canada has much in common with that of the U.S. but is also quite different. The most common types of retirement savings in Canada are Registered Retirement Savings Plans and pensions. Pensions work the same as in the U.S. in that the employer is generally liable to pay the employee a retirement benefit based on a formula, including things such as tenure, income history, and age. As in the U.S., pensions have become less common in Canada, but they are still more prevalent than in the U.S.

An RRSP is like an IRA or a 401(k). It is an account that working people can use to defer income. There are individual RRSPs you can set up yourself, and group RRSPs which are sponsored by an employer. Regardless of whether you use an individual plan or group plan, the contribution limit is the same. This is unlike in the U.S., where 401(k) deductibility limits are much higher than for IRAs. For this reason, I usually recommend clients use an individual RRSP unless the employer makes matching contributions to the group RRSP.

Using your own RRSP will give you more privacy, flexibility, and investment options. The RRSP contribution limit is 18% of your earned income from the previous year, up to the annual maximum, which is $32,490 in 2025. Once you report earned income to the Canada Revenue Agency (CRA) on your tax return, it creates RRSP "room". Those moving to Canada will not have any RRSP room in the year they arrive and hence will not be able to deduct any RRSP contributions.

RRSP room is cumulative, so if you do not make the full contribution one year, the unused portion rolls into the next year. The unused RRSP room is added to the new room that is created through your employment income in the previous year. This is different from the U.S. system, as 401(k) and IRA contributions have annual limits that are not cumulative. This is a nice feature because I have had clients who move from Canada to the U.S. who have $200,000 CAD or more in RRSP room. This means they did not do proper tax planning in previous years. However, having the extra RRSP room was very helpful in reducing their deemed disposition tax upon exit.

In the U.S., it is common for people to roll their 401(k) into an IRA once they retire or switch employers, but it is not required. You can leave your 401(k) at your former employer if they allow it and take your retirement income from there. One of the differences between the Canadian and U.S. retirement systems is that in Canada you are required to transfer your RRSP to a Registered Retirement Income Fund once you reach the age when minimum distributions are required. This has the same effect as the Required Minimum Distribution rules in the U.S. but requires the movement of money to a new account. You must transfer the funds in your RRSP to a RRIF by December 31st of the year you turn 71. Distributions from your RRIF must start by the end of the following year at age 72[52].

In the U.S., your money is your money and you can take it when you want. One significant difference is that Canada has locked-in retirement savings accounts, in addition to the regular retirement savings accounts such as RRSPs and RRIFs. A few of the common locked-in accounts are LIRAs, LIFs and Locked-in Retirement Income Funds (LRIFs). These types of accounts have a minimum distribution schedule like an IRA or RRIF, but they limit your maximum withdrawal[53].

Locked-in accounts are usually the result of rolling an employer pension into an individual account. The idea behind locking the account is to make sure people do not spend all their money too early and have some left for later in life. You can roll your U.S. pension into an IRA and then take distributions as you please. Your Canadian pension must roll into another locked-in account which will limit your distributions.

The periodic income from a LIF or LRIF is subject to annual minimum[54] and

---

[52] https://www.taxtips.ca/rrsp/converting-your-rrsp-to-a-rrif.htm

[53] https://www.fool.ca/investing/what-is-a-locked-in-retirement-account-lira/

[54] https://www.canada.ca/en/revenue-agency/services/tax/businesses/topics/completing-sli ps-summaries/t4rsp-t4rif-information-returns/payments/chart-prescribed-factors.html

maximum[55] withdrawal limits. As of 2025, Quebec no longer has a maximum LIF withdrawal for those age 55 or older[56]. The accounts are regulated by federal or provincial pension legislation depending on the plan from which the LIRA originated.

The minimum annual withdrawal amount is determined under Canada's Income Tax Regulations. The maximum annual withdrawal amount is determined under the Pension Benefits Standards Regulations of 1985. The maximum annual withdrawal limit is designed so that the account will not be depleted before the age of 89.

The maximum for provincially regulated LIFs and LRIFs is usually the greater of:

· The investment gains from the account in the previous calendar year; or
· An amount determined by multiplying the balance at the beginning of the year by a prescribed annuity factor.

If your LIF or LRIF is federally regulated, the percentages in the table from the website of the Office of the Superintendent of Financial Institutions (OSFI) can be used to determine the maximum annual withdrawal for the year. The percentages in the table change each year based on Canadian bond yields. The maximum withdrawal is not much higher than the minimum withdrawal in the early years. Initially, you may find that your locked-in fund grows each year, even if you are taking out the maximum amount.

Earlier, I named a few of the many types of retirement accounts available in Canada. The type of account used is generally determined by the province the

---

[55] https://www.osfi-bsif.gc.ca/en/supervision/pensions/administering-pension-plans/guidance-topic/life-income-funds-restricted-life-income-funds-variable-benefits-accounts

[56] https://www.taxtips.ca/pensions/rpp/lif-and-lrif-minimum-and-maximum-withdrawals.htm

account is in, how funds are contributed to the account, and how the funds are to be distributed. For example, when someone leaves an employer where they were earning a pension, the lump-sum commuted pension value can be transferred to a LIRA, if the person has not yet reached the age of 71 and does not want to start mandatory distributions yet.

Once the person is ready to start annuitizing their pension, they must transfer the funds again to a LIF or annuity. Distributions from a LIF must begin in the year after the funds arrive. LIRAs allow funds to be held without distributions. To recap, the funds would go from the employer pension to a LIRA to be invested, and then to a LIF to be distributed. Similarly, a RRSP is transferred to a RRIF to be distributed. There are accounts designed for the accumulation of funds, and then those funds are transferred to accounts used for distribution. To be designated a LIRA, the money must come from a pension plan, and the employer must be under provincial jurisdiction. If the pension plan is under federal jurisdiction (banks, telecommunications, aviation, and others), it's called a locked-in RRSP[57].

Most Canadian provinces allow non-residents to unlock their locked-in registered retirement accounts. Each province has its own rules, but generally this can be done after two years of non-residency[58]. Some provinces allow for the continued deferral of that income by allowing participants to transfer funds from their locked-in account to an RRSP; others do not. For example, Ontario allows non-residents to unlock their accounts after two years of non-residency, but it only allows those funds to be distributed to a LIF or as cash, not sent directly to an RRSP[59]. You cannot open a LIF until you are 55 years of age in most cases. You must begin minimum distributions once the funds

---

[57] https://www.savvynewcanadians.com/lira-lrsp-lif-lrif-rlif-prif-meaning/

[58] https://www.osfi-bsif.gc.ca/en/supervision/pensions/administering-pension-plans/guidance-topic/unlocking-funds-pension-plan-or-locked-retirement-savings-plan

[59] https://www.fsrao.ca/consumers/pensions/events-may-affect-your-pension/withdrawing-locked-accounts-because-financial-hardship

are in the LIF. If you open a LIF, you can transfer up to 50% of the account balance to an RRSP within 60 days of account opening. This will allow you to defer tax on half of the account, but you will have to start taking minimum distributions the following year.

The CRA is typically notified of your non-resident status when you file your "exit return" in the year you leave Canada, which must be filed by April 30th of the following year. There is a line on the return where you can notify the CRA of your departure date. Custodians will not accept your tax return as proof that the CRA has accepted your non-resident status. Custodians generally require that you obtain verification of your non-resident status from the CRA.

To unlock your locked-in retirement account, you will need to file Form NR-73 with the CRA[60]. The CRA will then issue you a Determination Letter verifying your non-resident status. You then submit the Determination Letter to the custodian, along with your request to unlock the account. Make sure to include directions to send the funds directly to your RRSP if allowed in your province. If a cheque is mistakenly issued to you personally, the entire amount may be taxable in that year.

Another effective retirement savings vehicle is a Tax-Free Savings Account (TFSA). TFSAs are like Roth IRAs in that contributions are not deductible, but funds grow tax-free once they are in the account. Investment income and distributions are not taxable. One important difference is that every Canadian taxpayer receives cumulative TFSA room each year ($7,000 in 2025).

In the U.S., your Roth IRA contributions are limited to your earned income or the annual limit, whichever is lower. You cannot make contributions if your income is above the threshold for the year. In 2025, your eligibility for contributing to a Roth IRA phases out between $236,000 and $246,000

---

[60] https://www.canada.ca/en/revenue-agency/services/forms-publications/forms/nr73.html

for joint filers[61]. TFSA "room" is cumulative, so if you do not make the full contribution, the unused room is added to your allotment for the following year[62]. TFSA distributions can be taken anytime tax-free, and you get the room back when you take a distribution. For example, if I had $20,000 in my TFSA and no additional room, and then took a $10,000 distribution, it would be added to my available room, so the following year my TFSA room would be $17,000. Roth IRA contributions have an annual limit regardless of your contribution in the previous year. The Roth IRA contribution limit is $7,000 USD in 2025, or $8,000 if the contributor is aged 50 or over.

Unlike the Roth IRA, the TFSA was not included in the Canada-U.S. Tax Treaty, so they are taxed like a brokerage account for U.S. taxpayers. The Roth IRA is a great planning tool for those moving to Canada. TFSAs can still be beneficial for U.S. taxpayers living in Canada because TFSAs allow them to defer provincial tax as well. U.S. citizens living in Canada will have to pay income tax in the U.S. on investment income in their TFSA, but they will pay less tax because the account is tax-free in Canada.

Filing Form 3520 with the IRS is no longer required for TFSAs, RESPs, or RDSPs. Those moving to the U.S. should close their TFSA shortly before leaving Canada. The distribution is not taxable and closing the account will simplify your life. Keeping the account open will make your life more difficult for several reasons:

- It is another account to manage.
- It makes your taxes more complicated.
- Reporting the income correctly will be difficult because the custodian will not be creating tax slips like a 1099 or T5 because the income is not

---

[61] https://www.irs.gov/newsroom/401k-limit-increases-to-23500-for-2025-ira-limit-remains-7000

[62] https://www.canada.ca/en/revenue-agency/news/newsroom/tax-tips/tax-tips-2021/understanding-tax-free-savings-account-tfsa.html

taxable in Canada.

Lastly, there is no such thing as a "TFSA conversion" like there is for Roth IRAs. In the U.S., when funds are distributed from an IRA, an exception is allowed for the contribution of an equal amount to a Roth IRA. In other words, the annual Roth IRA contribution limit does not apply if you take a distribution from an IRA in the same year. The CRA does not allow for equal contributions to your TFSA when distributing funds from your RRSP or other registered account. The TFSA contribution limit does not change based on income or distributions from other accounts. From a planning perspective, Canadian residents who are not U.S. taxpayers should utilize all their TFSA room before they invest in taxable accounts.

Estate planning considerations are different in Canada than they are in the U.S. When someone dies in the U.S., they can pass their IRA or Roth IRA to their heirs, who can then distribute it over 10 years[63]. Canada has a deemed disposition tax when someone dies. They can pass their registered accounts to their spouse without any immediate taxation. The surviving spouse can then treat that account as their own. All your taxable accounts are deemed disposed of upon your passing away, but the deemed disposition can be deferred until your spouse's death if the account is passed to them[64]. All your accounts will be deemed disposed of, or fully distributed, when the second spouse passes away.

A deemed disposition is when tax is required to be paid on capital gains from assets that have not been sold. In Canada, a deemed disposition takes place any time asset ownership changes, someone moves away from Canada, or

---

[63] https://www.irs.gov/retirement-plans/plan-participant-employee/retirement-topics-beneficiary

[64] https://www.bdo.ca/insights/tax-considerations-following-the-loss-of-a-spouse-or-common-law-partner-part-ii

a death occurs[65]. For taxable accounts, unrealized gains are taxed when a deemed disposition occurs. For registered retirement accounts, the account balance is fully taxable based on the date of death.

As you can see, the lowest tax bracket is 50% higher than in the U.S. (15% vs. 10%). Canada's tax brackets are also more compressed, meaning you pay higher tax rates at lower income levels. It is commonly believed that Canadian tax rates are higher than in the U.S. This is generally true, and most people will pay more income tax in Canada, but the top two federal tax brackets in the U.S. are higher than the top bracket in Canada.

CANADA

2025 Taxable Income	Rate
first $57,375	14.50%
$57,375 - $114,750	20.50%
$114,750 - $177,882	26.00%
$177,882 - $253,414	29.31%
over $253,414	33.00%

UNITED STATES

---

[65] https://www.taxtips.ca/glossary/deemed-disposition.htm

Tax rate	Single filer	Married filing jointly (or surviving spouse)	Head of household	Married filing separately
10%	$0 to $11,925	$0 to $23,850	$0 to $17,000	$0 to $11,925
12%	$11,926 to $48,475	$23,851 to $96,950	$17,001 to $64,850	$11,926 to $48,475
22%	$48,476 to $103,350	$96,951 to $206,700	$64,851 to $103,350	$48,476 to $103,350
24%	$103,351 to $197,300	$206,701 to $394,600	$103,351 to $197,300	$103,351 to $197,300
32%	$197,301 to $250,525	$394,601 to $501,050	$197,301 to $250,500	$197,301 to $250,525
35%	$250,526 to $626,350	$501,051 to $751,600	$250,501 to $626,350	$250,526 to $375,800
37%	$626,351 or more	$751,601 or more	$626,351 or more	$375,801 or more

Also, Canada does not have the additional taxes that many high-income earners in the U.S. must pay, such as the AMT, NIIT, or Medicare Surtax. Additionally, Canada has some other programs, such as the Canada Child Benefit, which is a monthly payment made to qualifying parents of minors to offset the cost of raising children. This benefit is potentially larger than the Child Tax Credit in the U.S. Most people will pay more federal income tax in Canada, but the difference may not be as large as you imagine, particularly when the cost of healthcare in the U.S. is included.

Provincial income tax in Canada is generally much higher than state income tax in the U.S. There are some U.S. states with no income tax while every Canadian province has an income tax. In the U.S., the highest state income tax rate belongs to California, with 13.3%. This rate is much higher than that of the state with the next highest rate: Hawaii, with 11%. These are the only two U.S. states with double-digit income tax brackets. In California, joint tax filers do not hit the top tax bracket until their income reaches $1 million. Using the long-term average exchange rate of approximately $1.25 CAD/USD, that income level is equivalent to $1.25 million in Canada.

The Canadian province with the highest income tax rate is Quebec, with a top tax rate of 25.75%[66]. This rate must be paid on all income over $129,590 CAD in 2025 (equivalent to $103,672 USD). Nova Scotia and New Brunswick also have income tax rates above 20%. The territory with the lowest income tax

---

[66] https://www.taxtips.ca/taxrates/qc.htm

rate is Nunavut, at 11.5%[67]. Most of the provinces have top income tax rates that are in the mid-teens[68]. All the provinces have top tax brackets that begin at much lower income levels than in any of the U.S. states.

Much of the differences when comparing tax liabilities in Canada and the U.S. are at the provincial and state level. A large reason for the higher provincial income tax rates compared to those of the states is because of provincial healthcare programs. Healthcare expenses in Canada are minimal, whereas health insurance premiums are a significant expense in the U.S., and deductibles and other costs can also be expensive.

Because of the deemed disposition and the higher tax rates, it is important to consider overall taxation when designing distribution strategies for registered accounts in Canada. If you live in Quebec and have a large RRSP when you die, most of that account will be taxed at rates as high as 53.31% in the year of your death or your surviving spouse's death.

Most of the provinces have combined tax rates that are above 50% when local and surtaxes are included[69]. This should be avoided if possible because most people deduct those contributions at lower tax rates while they are working. You do not want to deduct income at a lower rate than that at which the distribution is taxed.

Remember, you are not losing the money that is distributed from a retirement account. You must pay tax on the distribution, but the funds can be immediately reinvested in your taxable brokerage account or TFSA. Early distributions do create a tax drag on your portfolio, but they should be considered if they will result in you paying a lower tax rate. The rate difference must justify the

---

[67] https://www.taxtips.ca/taxrates/nu.htm

[68] https://www.nerdwallet.com/ca/personal-finance/provincial-tax-rates

[69] https://www.taxtips.ca/taxrates/taxcomparison/2020-tax-comparison-employment-inco me.htm

tax drag.

For example, if I pay 12% on a $100 distribution from my RRSP, I lose that $12 to tax and will not earn any investment income on those funds. The remaining $88 can go into my TFSA and never be taxed again. The $12 I lost to tax is what I am referring to as tax drag. I will have less overall investment income because my account balance is lower. I may still come out ahead if my tax rate goes up in the future. The tax rate difference must justify the tax drag.

There are a lot of factors that go into tax planning distribution decisions, such as if you have a spouse, where and how the funds will be invested after distribution, your spouse's tax bracket, and other forms of income you and your spouse have. You also do not know how long you will live, so you cannot be certain of the distribution period. Many financial decisions involve assumptions that may not come to fruition. Do not get stuck in analysis paralysis. All you can do is make the best decision you can based on all available information.

Unlike qualified retirement accounts in the U.S., registered retirement accounts in Canada do not have early withdrawal penalties. There is a 10% penalty tax in the U.S. for non-qualified IRA distributions taken before age $59\frac{1}{2}$[70].

As mentioned previously, before decisions can be made about early RRSP distributions or Roth conversions, you need to know approximately what your lifetime cash flows and annual tax liability will be. If you know you will be in a higher tax bracket in your later years because of minimum retirement account distributions and pensions, you should consider taking money out early at a lower tax rate.

---

[70] https://www.irs.gov/retirement-plans/plan-participant-employee/retirement-topics-exceptions-to-tax-on-early-distributions

Granted, much of this exercise is a gamble on your life expectancy. We could do your tax planning perfectly if we knew exactly when you would die. We do not have that information, so we have to make some educated guesses based on life expectancy, medical history, and family history. If you believe you have a shortened life expectancy, you should be more aggressive in getting your money out of registered retirement accounts earlier in retirement.

Canada gives self-employed people a nice opportunity for income deferral and preferred tax rates in retirement through Canadian-Controlled Private Corporations (CCPCs)[71]. Essentially, those who are self-employed or private contractors can set up their own personal corporation to receive their employment income. The corporation pays corporate tax on the money as it is received. The money can then either be retained in the corporation and invested, or it can be distributed to the owner in the form of dividends subject to the dividend tax structure. The federal tax rate on CCPCs is 9% on income up to the business limit of $500,000. Income above that level is taxed at 15%[72].

Also, these preferred tax rates are limited for corporations with too much capital. The business limit is reduced by $100,000 for every $1 million the corporation has in capital over $10 million, until it is eliminated at $15 million. In other words, CCPCs can have up to $10 million in retained capital without affecting their business limit ($500,000). If a corporation has $15 million or more in retained capital, none of its income will qualify for CCPC tax rates regardless of the income level, and all profits are taxed at 15% (federal). This calculation is subject to change as a new measure has received royal ascent and will change the way the business limit reduction is calculated.

Lastly, the business limit can be reduced based on investment income. CCPCs

---

[71] https://www.canada.ca/en/revenue-agency/services/tax/businesses/topics/corporations/type-corporation.html

[72] https://www.canada.ca/en/revenue-agency/services/tax/businesses/topics/corporations/corporation-tax-rates.html

can have up to $50,000 in investment income with no reduction in their business limit. Above $50,000 in investment income, the business limit is reduced by approximately $125,000 for each additional $25,000 in investment income. The business limit is eliminated when investment income reaches $150,000.

A CCPC's passive income business limit reduction for a particular taxation year will be the amount determined by the formula:

BL/$500,000 x 5 (AAII - $50,000)

Where:

BL is the CCPC's business limit otherwise determined for the particular year (i.e., its business limit as described above); and

AAII is the total of all amounts each of which is the adjusted aggregate investment income of the CCPC, or of any corporations with which it is associated at any time in the particular year, for each of their taxation years that ended in the preceding calendar year[73].

The provincial tax rates for CCPC income range from 0% to 5%, resulting in total corporate tax of 9% to 20% depending on which province the business operates in, how much income it generates, how much capital it retains, and how much investment income is generated from retained capital.

Investment income within CCPCs is taxed more punitively. The federal tax rate for CCPC investment income is 38.7%, and the provincial rates vary from 10% to 16%[74]. Investment income within a CCPC can result in total tax of between

---

[73] https://www.canada.ca/en/revenue-agency/programs/about-canada-revenue-agency-cra/federal-government-budgets/budget-2018-equality-growth-strong-middle-class/passive-investment-income/small-business-deduction-rules.html

[74] https://kpmg.com/ca/en/home/services/tax/tax-facts/canadian-corporate-tax-tables.html

48.67% and 54.7%. Only half of capital gains is taxable. Dividend taxation for corporations gets quite complex in Canada. Dividends from a connected corporation are tax-free. Dividends from non-connected corporations are grossed up and have a tax credit applied, but they are beyond the scope of this book.

What complicates corporate dividend income more than personal dividend income is the involvement of a Refundable Dividend Tax on Hand (RDTOH) account, a Non-Eligible RDTOH (NERDTOH) account and a Capital Dividend Account (CDA)[75]. These are notional (hypothetical) accounts that regulate how much income can be distributed to the owner tax-free as a return of capital. For these reasons, CCPCs are primarily used for tax deferral on active business income. For most owners, there is no advantage to investing funds within the CCPC when compared to investing in their individual account. The CCPC investment income tax rates are like those of the top individual tax bracket.

Pensions are currently more common in Canada than the U.S. They work the same in both countries where the employer is liable to pay a retirement benefit to the employee based on a benefit formula. The employee does not contribute to the plan. Their benefit is based on things like age at initiation of benefits, number of years as a plan member, average pay, final pay, and distribution option (e.g. joint life). If you can afford to delay receipt of pension benefits, it is likely you should consider rolling the pension into your LIRA instead.

Having a large pension usually means you will not have a large RRSP balance. Since pension contributions are not taxable to the employee, the CRA does not want to let people "double up" and make full RRSP contributions also. To prevent this, employer pension contributions result in a pension adjustment,

---

[75] https://www.canada.ca/en/revenue-agency/programs/about-canada-revenue-agency-cra/
federal-government-budgets/budget-2018-equality-growth-strong-middle-class/passive
-investment-income/dividend-refund-rules.html

which is a reduction in your RRSP room[76]. Many people who have pensions are left with a small amount of RRSP room each year. Highly paid employees and executives rarely have any RRSP room after the pension adjustment.

Many people who retire in Canada have a savings account, taxable investments, RRSPs, LIRAs and a TFSA. Married couples can have 10 or more sources of retirement income. So how do you decide the order in which to tap your income sources to minimize taxes over your lifetime? This decision is a little easier in Canada because all retirement account distributions are fully taxable except for your TFSA. Also, there are no CPP spousal benefits or Roth conversions.

TFSA balances are usually relatively small because the account was not introduced until 2009 so the maximum total TFSA contribution is $102,000 through 2025. Most people do not make all their TFSA contributions and many do not have their TFSA invested in equities. The majority invest the funds in money markets or Guaranteed Investment Contracts (GICs) because most TFSAs are held at brick-and-mortar retail banks. What is the point of investing in a TFSA if you are not going to generate any income? Although interest rates have gone up, the rates retail banks offer are still low compared to the potential returns of a well-diversified portfolio.

The one thing that does complicate retirement cash-flow sequencing in Canada is the fact that married spouses file separate tax returns. This presents the opportunity for income splitting. Since each spouse files his or her own return, you want their taxable incomes to be as close as possible to each other's each year. By avoiding having one spouse in a low tax bracket and the other in a much higher bracket, both spouses are more likely to be in lower tax brackets. This will result in a lower combined tax liability.

---

[76] https://www.canada.ca/en/revenue-agency/services/forms-publications/publications/t408
4/pension-adjustment-guide.html

Canada's Income Attribution Rules limit income splitting opportunities[77]. Income splitting should be done over many years. Also, there are some opportunities built into the tax code through pension splitting and use of the "spousal amount"[78]. The spousal amount allows a lower-income spouse to transfer any of their unused "personal amount" (an indexed amount that is given to each taxpayer to reduce their annual taxes) onto their higher-income spouse's tax return.

The CRA allows you to opt to split certain pension income on your tax return. Nothing changes with the pension payments, but your spouse may be able to put a portion (up to half) of the income on their tax return rather than yours. This can be done with many traditional pensions including SS, 401(k)s, and other employer provided pensions, but not with IRAs or OAS. CPP credits can be split upon separation or divorce[79]. Your CPP benefits can be shared with your spouse based on the amount of time you lived together after the age of 18[80].

I mentioned when discussing U.S. retirement income that the income tax bracket of heirs should be considered for those in the later stages of life, because their IRA funds will have to be distributed over a 10-year period after their death if inherited by anyone other than their spouse. Some IRA owners in their late 80s and 90s may want to consider taking bigger IRA distributions than they need if their heirs will pay significantly higher tax rates as Canadian residents once the IRA is inherited.

This complication does not exist in Canada because only spouses can inherit

---

[77] https://www.taxtips.ca/personaltax/attribution-rules-re-gifts-transfers-loans-to-spouse-or-related-minor-child.htm

[78] https://www.canada.ca/en/revenue-agency/services/tax/individuals/topics/about-your-tax-return/tax-return/completing-a-tax-return/deductions-credits-expenses/line-30300-spouse-common-law-partner-amount.html

[79] https://www.canada.ca/en/services/benefits/publicpensions/cpp/cpp-split-credits.html

[80] https://www.canada.ca/en/services/benefits/publicpensions/cpp/share-cpp.html

registered accounts without a deemed disposition. If anyone but your spouse is the beneficiary of your LIRA or RRSP, the account will be fully distributed on the date of your death and all that income will be included on your final tax return, with few exceptions. This is Canada's version of an estate tax, but it results in more taxable income in the year of your death and there is no exemption amount.

As with government benefits, you have to gamble on your life expectancy when doing tax planning. If you believe you have a shortened life expectancy, you should consider taking larger distributions than necessary from your registered accounts to avoid having a large balance exposed to the deemed disposition tax at the top marginal tax rate. In this situation, we still want to defer tax for as long as possible, so you should never take unnecessary distributions at the top tax rate. Only take distributions for tax purposes if you will be paying a lower tax rate that justifies paying the tax earlier than necessary.

The last factor that can complicate retirement income sequencing is a significant age difference between spouses. I am referring to those who have an age difference of five years or more. First, this may mean that one spouse is retired for many years while the other is still working. Ideally, this would mean the retired spouse would not need to take any retirement income for living expenses and can let their government pensions grow along with their retirement account balances.

For those who are wealthy, it may be best to take some distributions from your retirement accounts when you do not need to so you can take advantage of lower tax brackets. It is a similar concept to the Roth conversion except the funds are deposited into a taxable account or TFSA. Since you file separate tax returns, the income of your spouse will not affect you beyond the potential spousal amount and any income-splitting elections made.

If both spouses are retiring at the same time but there is a significant age difference, should you both take equal amounts of income? Or should you each take amounts that are proportionate to your account balances? The younger spouse can obviously defer income for longer, but should they?

The younger spouse has more years to take early distributions to potentially decrease future taxable distributions. The older spouse is likely to pass away first, which means the surviving spouse will likely inherit financial assets and will begin receiving government pension survivor benefits for SS and CPP. The surviving spouse's taxable income will increase after the first spouse's death and all their combined RRSP balances will be fully taxable on their final tax return. All this will need to be accounted for when you do your tax planning.

There are four primary ways income splitting can be achieved:

1. When there is a significant difference in the income of spouses, the higher-income spouse should be contributing to a spousal RRSP while the lower-earning spouse contributes to their own RRSP up to their limit. If the lower-earning spouse has little income, they should fund their TFSA first and may not want to use an RRSP. The higher-income spouse should also fund their own TFSA and pay for all the family's living expenses. The higher-earning spouse will have larger government pensions, so it may be better if the lower-earning spouse ends up with more assets in their name (spousal RRSP). There are no rules around who must pay for living expenses, which creates an opportunity for income splitting through adjusting saving and spending patterns.

2. Gifting while residents of the U.S., before becoming Canadian tax residents. You must be aware of the U.S. gifting laws, which restrict how much can be gifted to a non-resident, non-citizen (alien) spouse, which is $190,000 in 2025. Above that amount you will be required to file a U.S. gift tax return Form 709, and your lifetime estate tax exemption amount will be reduced by the amount gifted above the annual limit. Resident aliens (non-citizens) receive the full estate and gift tax exemption, so gifting between spouses should be done while you are both U.S. residents.

3. Make the pension splitting election on your tax return once you are taking distributions. Some pensions are eligible for splitting; some are not. SS and OAS cannot be split or shared between married or common-law couples. Most employer-sponsored defined benefit plans, defined contribution plans, RRIFs, life annuities and IRAs qualify for pension splitting on the tax return. The election to split income is done on Form T1032 – *Joint Election to Split Pension Income.*

4. Canadians have the option of using their own age, or their spouse's age[81], when calculating minimum RRIF withdrawals. Use the younger spouse's age when figuring out minimum RRIF withdrawals. This will result in lower minimum RRIF payments. You can still take out as much as you want, but this gives you more flexibility. Here is the formula for calculating minimum RRIF withdrawals for those under 71 (after 1992):

(1/(90-age at beginning of year)) x FMV of RRIF at beginning of year[82].

Beginning at 71, there is a distribution table like that used for IRA RMDs.

The reason I say using your spouse's age for RRIF withdrawals is a form of income splitting is because if the older spouse has higher income, it allows them to reduce their taxable income. It also means the couple will rely more on the income of the lower- income spouse for living expenses. If they require more income for living expenses, they can take those distributions from the lower-income spouse's registered accounts. The older spouse is also likely to pass away earlier, and the younger spouse will inherit their registered assets. This allows the younger spouse to take income that the older spouse would have otherwise had to take earlier while they were alive.

---

[81] https://www.canada.ca/en/revenue-agency/services/tax/businesses/topics/completing-slips-summaries/t4rsp-t4rif-information-returns/payments/minimum-amount-a-rrif.html

[82] https://www.taxtips.ca/rrsp/rrif-minimum-withdrawals.htm

In the case of the first two points above, the income splitting must be done before you reach retirement. There are three things that can be done to effectively split income after you stop working. You should use the higher-income spouse's taxable accounts before the lower-income spouse's taxable accounts. I am not saying you should distribute taxable accounts first, as this may not be the case. I am simply referring to which spouse's taxable account is distributed first.

If you need extra spending money outside of your regular budget or distribution schedule, use the higher-income spouse's taxable account first. This strategy does not split income in the current year, but it will reduce the higher-income spouse's account balances faster, leading to less investment income being subject to higher tax rates. Of course, capital gains need to be considered, as taking large capital gains could be counterproductive.

With income splitting, you are more limited once you stop working. Those who are wealthy and have low living expenses may want to take larger distributions and pay more taxes than needed early in retirement to avoid a larger deemed disposition at death. When you have a long-term view and you look at the big picture of how much money you and your heirs are left with versus how much tax you pay before and after your death, it may be better to pay more tax now than necessary. Even if you and your heirs are both in lower tax brackets, a large deemed disposition could push most of your assets into the top tax bracket if they are all taxed at the same time.

The time value of money is based on the discount rate, which is usually the expected return on your portfolio for this type of calculation. I recommend being conservative in your assumption of portfolio returns because it is better to be safe than sorry. I would rather have my additional distributions be too low than too high, and your risk tolerance is likely to get more conservative as you age. This means you will have less equity exposure and should expect lower long-term returns.

From a financial planning perspective, making financial projections requires the use of assumptions. For example, we do not know what future rates of return will be or how tax rates might change. Assumptions and reality rarely match, so projections must be updated regularly. Proposed legislation gives a preview of how things may change in the future, but most legislation does not become law for one reason or another. If nothing else, it gives us a glimpse into what politicians are thinking.

That said, we can only plan using what we know. I use current tax law, current treaty language, and conservative historical rates of return on investments. The inflation rate I use for base scenarios is 2% because that is the stated target average inflation rate for the Federal Reserve Bank Open Market Committee[83]. I then run alternative scenarios varying inflation and other inputs.

The best way to do cash-flow sequencing for tax planning is to map your lifetime cash flows and tax liability. Software may be required to do this accurately. Those who are experienced with Excel and taxation may be able to put together a spreadsheet for this on their own, but most people will need help from a professional. Accuracy is important because small errors can change results exponentially over time.

What I usually see when projecting retirement income for those who have large retirement account balances, and assuming positive return on investment, is their account balances grow for the first several years after retirement because they are only taking out what they need to supplement their other income. At age 72, they are required to start taking minimum RRIF distributions. In that year they will have to take a distribution of approximately 5.4% of the account balance. Their portfolio may still be growing at this time if returns are good. The percentage that must be taken out goes up each year so that you must take out about 10% of your account balance at age 88 and about 20% at age 95.

---

[83] https://www.federalreserve.gov/newsevents/pressreleases/monetary20200827a.htm

Upon retirement, most people move from a higher income-tax bracket into one of the bottom brackets. Then from age 70 onwards, their tax bracket increases because of government pensions and minimum distributions. When deciding when to initiate your various retirement income sources, here are the general principles to go by in Canada:

1. Maximize government pensions if possible.
2. Defer income for as long as possible unless you can take it out earlier at a lower tax rate.
3. Align income with your spouse's as much as possible.
4. Plan your cash flows so that your tax rate stays consistent throughout your lifetime.
5. Remember there will be a deemed disposition upon your death (or the death of your spouse). If generational wealth transfer is important to you, planning should be done during your lifetime to distribute more funds than needed for your own personal tax planning, to ensure you do not have a large deemed disposition taxed at rates of 50% or more. Most people want to pass as much as possible to their heirs and pay as little tax as possible.

Because there is a deemed disposition in Canada, the top combined tax rates are higher, and the tax brackets are more compressed, you should ensure your RRSP and other registered account balances are down to between $400,000 and $500,000 by the time you are 85 or so, if you have enough other income and assests. You do not want to take out too much while you are alive so that you drain your RRSP and have no RRSP income included in your final income tax return. You also do not want to pass away with $1 million in your RRSP to then have a $400,000 to $500,000 bill on your final tax return.

The tax liability of your brokerage account is dependent on the allocation of the account, the balance, and market returns. The only way to reduce the taxation on this account is to change the allocation or reduce the balance. TFSAs should be used for unplanned spending so that taking the extra distribution does not negatively impact your tax planning. Accounts should be consolidated as much as possible. Your cash-flow planning should be updated annually to account for changes. Once you have your cash flows mapped, the only thing left to do is to be diligent and ensure you execute the planning you have done.

6

Cross-Border

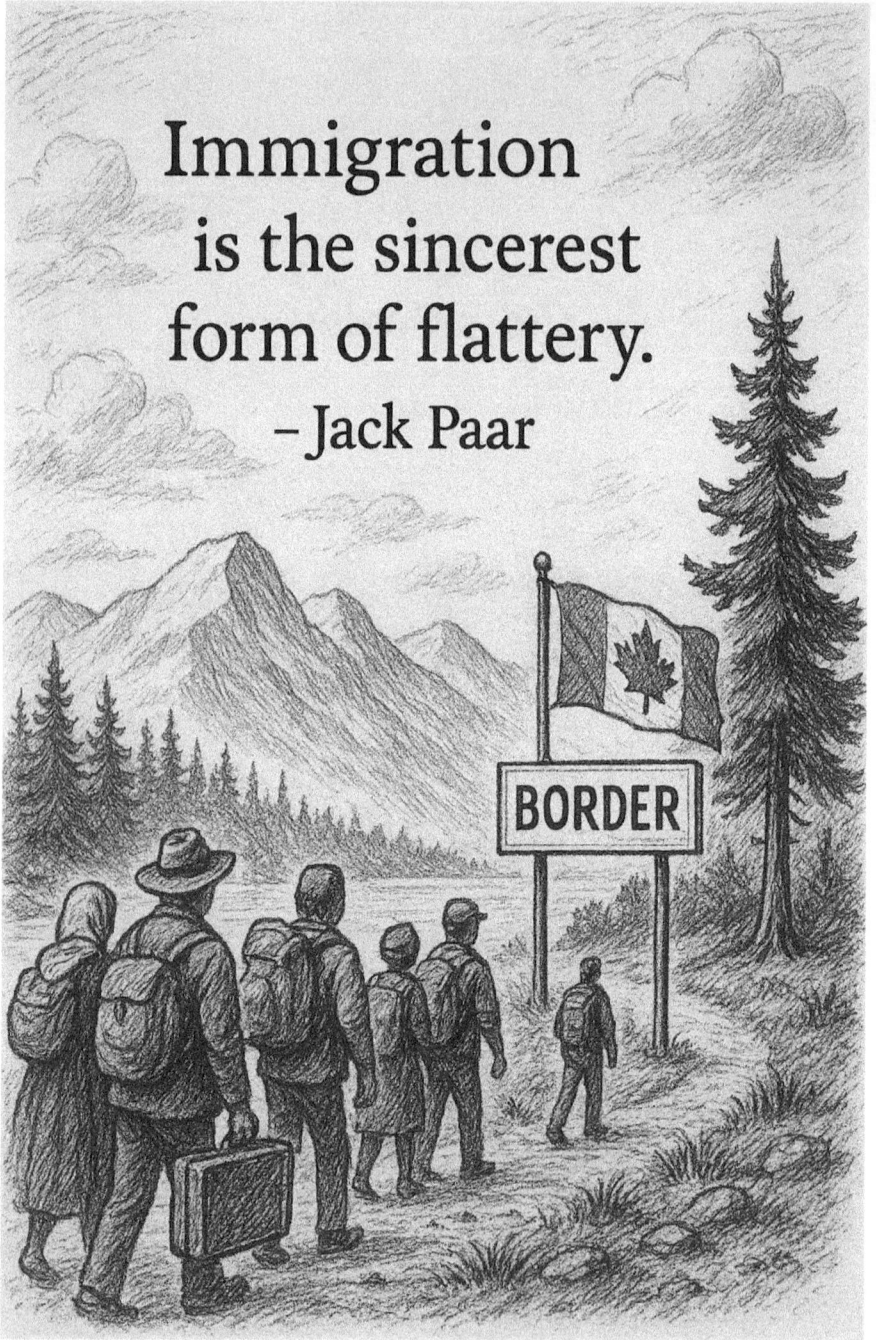

Immigration
is the sincerest
form of flattery.
– Jack Paar

If you have lived and worked in both Canada and the U.S., you qualify for SS, CPP, and OAS. You may have retirement assets as well as taxable investments in both countries, and in both currencies. You have decided where you are going to spend your retirement years and now you need to decide the most tax efficient way to generate income to support your lifestyle. When should you take your government pensions? Which accounts should you take distributions from, and in which order?

Without getting off on too much of a tangent, cross-border financial, tax, and investment planning can get quite complex. If you have $1 million or more in your portfolio, it is in your best interest to hire a cross-border specialist. Some people may not mind spending a significant amount of time trying to figure out how to do this on their own. Most of the information you need can be found on the internet. The problem is, you cannot know what questions to ask if you do not do this for a living. It is possible to figure out most of the issues on your own. However, making a mistake in this context can lead to tax penalties, fines, paying more tax than necessary or having significant opportunity losses.

As a simple example, I have met many people who did not know they qualify for OAS because of the Social Security Totalization Agreement between Canada and the U.S.[84] For someone eligible for a benefit of $200 per month, that is $36,000 of free money they would miss out on if they started taking benefits at 65 and lived to be 80, not including the time value of money or cost of living adjustments.

You have heard the saying "Mo money, mo problems". That is usually true; the more money you have, the more complex your situation gets and the more financial planning opportunities you have. The opportunities and complexity are multiplied in a cross-border context. It took me about three and a half years of working in cross-border financial planning, earning the U.S. and

---

[84] https://www.ssa.gov/international/Agreement_Pamphlets/canada.html

Canadian CFP® marks, and preparing U.S. and Canadian tax returns before I felt like I really knew what I was doing. Working with a knowledgeable and well-rounded expert helps ensure that opportunities are not missed, and mistakes are not made.

Why not work with two teams – a CFP® and CPA in the U.S. and a CFP® and CPA/CA in Canada? These advisors are likely good at their job in their respective countries. They could work together to collaborate from each of their perspectives. The Canada-U.S. Tax Treaty supersedes domestic tax law in both countries. Unless one of your advisors has practiced in both countries and knows how to apply the Treaty, mistakes will be made, and opportunities will be missed.

Unfortunately, there is no class or program you can take to learn the Canada-U.S. Tax Treaty. The only way to know it well is to study and apply it. Additionally, it is uncommon for advisors who do not work for the same firm to collaborate as much as necessary. Even if you can get your Canada and U.S. advisors on the phone together to coordinate, it will not do much good if neither of them has the cross-border knowledge.

Why don't more advisors practice in both countries? For most fee-only wealth management firms, much of their revenue comes from asset management fees. Each country has their own rules and regulations around what is required to manage assets. Generally, there is a minimum education or licensing standard, as well as a requirement to be registered in the state or provinces you will be practicing in. In the U.S., the minimum requirement to transact securities trades is a Series 6 or Series 7 license. To manage assets, you must be an Investment Advisor Representative for a Registered Investment Advisor, which requires a Series 65 license. In Canada, you must obtain the Chartered Investment Manager (CIM) designation to manage assets.

You must also be registered as an investment manager in both countries. In the U.S., you can either register with the Securities Exchange Commission

(SEC) or you can be registered with the states, depending on how much the firm has in assets under management (AUM). Generally, firms with over $100 million USD AUM must register with the SEC. Smaller firms register in their state(s) of business. U.S. firms are subject to audit by their regulating body (SEC or state), which usually happens every few years.

In Canada, there is no national securities regulator. Each firm must register with one province being the primary regulator, as well as register with any other provinces where they do business. Every firm must also perform an independent audit each year. In this respect, it is harder to become a portfolio manager in Canada than the U.S. because the education requirements are slightly more stringent, there is a little more oversight, and business start-up costs and annual regulatory expenses are higher. Most advisors do not encounter enough potential clients with significant foreign assets to justify going through the hardship and expense of practicing in two countries. Most importantly, it requires rigorous training and years of experience to become a proficient advisor in two countries.

One reason why it is important to work with an advisor who practices on both sides of the border is for foreign tax credit planning. Both the IRS and CRA have a system of foreign tax credits to mitigate double taxation on the same income. There are two types of foreign tax credits in the U.S. Passive foreign tax credits are generated when there is foreign tax paid on passive income abroad. This includes interest, dividends, rents, royalties, and capital gains. General limitation foreign tax credits are generated when there is foreign tax paid on income not clearly fitting in the other categories. This could include active business income, employment wages, director's fees, or some pensions and annuities[85].

The U.S. foreign tax credit system is more complicated than Canada's. In the U.S., you have two options with your foreign tax credits: you can deduct them

---

[85] https://www.irs.gov/forms-pubs/about-publication-514

on Schedule A as an itemized deduction or keep them as a foreign tax credit. A credit is better than a deduction because a credit reduces your tax payable directly, whereas a deduction reduces your taxable income. This also reduces your tax payable, but only in proportion to your tax bracket. If taken as a deduction, the deduction must be taken in the same year the foreign tax is paid. There is no carryover of the deduction. You will not get the full benefit of the foreign tax credit and will experience double taxation. You cannot take a foreign tax credit and a deduction in the same year.

A deduction is not as beneficial as a credit but, in some cases, may be the only way to avoid some double taxation. If taken as a credit, you can only use foreign tax credits in proportion to how much tax the foreign income generates on your U.S. tax return. To accomplish this, the IRS has a formula that uses domestic income in relation to foreign income to determine the limit on foreign tax credits you can use in any tax year[86]. Also, income is divided into passive and general limitation, and foreign tax credits can only be used against the same type of income.

Foreign tax credits are first used in the year generated but can be carried back one year and then carried forward for up to 10 years. You want to minimize the amount of foreign tax credits you generate while maximizing the amount you use up. This is difficult in practice, but every dollar of credit used up or avoided eliminates a dollar of double taxation.

To the extent that you will be reporting worldwide income on both the U.S. and Canadian returns, it is important that both returns are prepared together or at the same time to optimize the foreign tax credits available and minimize double taxation. Canada does not differentiate the foreign tax credits and simply applies them to the foreign-sourced income. What gets tricky is U.S.-sourced income is taxed first by the IRS and then becomes a foreign tax credit

---

[86] https://www.irs.gov/individuals/international-taxpayers/foreign-tax-credit-how-to-figure-the-credit

on your Canadian return. Canada-sourced income is taxed first by the CRA and then becomes a foreign tax credit on your U.S. return.

Another complicating factor is that foreign tax credits cannot be used against all kinds of taxes that are generated on your income tax return. For example, the AMT carries its own foreign tax credits. Also, with the passing of the American Taxpayer Relief Act in 2013, additional surtax rates have now been imposed on high-earning individuals and families. The NIT is a 3.8% tax applied to passive income when MAGI is above $250,000 USD for joint filers[87]. The Medicare Surtax was added through the Affordable Care Act and is a 0.9% tax on earned income above $250,000 USD for joint filers[88]. The income threshold is not indexed for either of these taxes[89]. Foreign tax credits cannot be used to offset either tax.

Your life will automatically get much more complex when you move across an international border, especially if you have continued income or assets in your previous home. The first recommendation I would make to anyone preparing for this type of move is to simplify your life. One of the easiest ways to do this is to consolidate your accounts as much as possible. If you have multiple 401(k)s, roll them all into a Rollover IRA. Likewise, if you have multiple RRSPs or brokerage accounts, consolidate them to reduce the number of accounts you must keep track of or transfer over the border.

From a trading standpoint, consolidating accounts will help to reduce transaction charges, investment overlap and cash drag in the future. Having more accounts results in more transaction charges because there are more accounts to disperse the money into. Investment overlap means you hold the same investment in two different accounts. Cash drag occurs when there is residual

---

[87] https://www.irs.gov/individuals/net-investment-income-tax

[88] https://www.irs.gov/businesses/small-businesses-self-employed/questions-and-answers-for-the-additional-medicare-tax

[89] https://www.govinfo.gov/content/pkg/FR-2013-11-29/pdf/2013-28411.pdf

cash in the account after trading and fees. The more accounts you have, the more residual cash you will likely be left with.

The next step to planning retirement cash-flow sequencing is to map your cash flows throughout your life. As mentioned before, you do have to take a gamble on how long you will live in many respects. This is applicable with government pensions and will also affect Roth conversions and early retirement account distributions. It is best to make those decisions in the context of a greater overall plan.

You need to quantify each spouse's potential income throughout retirement before you can make any decisions on when and how to alter your distributions. You will need to update your plans annually because of investment performance and changes in the currency exchange rate. Also remember that if you retire early (before 60) there is no early withdrawal penalty on your RRSP. Early withdrawals from your IRA, before age 59½, will result in a 10% surtax penalty that should be avoided[90].

The taxation of your accounts changes when you move from Canada to the U.S. First, not all the U.S. states abide by the Canada-U.S. Tax Treaty, so some of them do not honor the tax deferral of registered accounts in Canada. Those moving to California, Delaware, Arkansas, Pennsylvania, or South Carolina will need to remember this at tax time because they will be required to pay state income tax on all investment income in those accounts. This will increase your tax burden and tax preparation fees.

It can also be difficult to determine what the income from the account is. The investment income is not taxable in Canada so the custodian will not issue a tax slip for the account unless there is a distribution. Any tax slip issued will report the distribution amount, not the investment income. The best way

---

90 https://www.irs.gov/newsroom/what-if-i-withdraw-money-from-my-ira#:~:text=Gener ally%2C%20early%20withdrawal%20from%20an,premium%20after%20a%20job%20loss

to determine the income for the year is to get a transaction history and find all the dividends, interest, and capital gains. Each income item should be converted to USD on the date received, which can create a significant amount of manual work.

This is complicated with capital gains because the currency exchange must be made when the security was both bought and sold. Some of the securities in the account may have been held for decades, so currency exchange rates will need to be pulled from many previous years. The custodian may not be able to provide you with the original purchase price. Most states follow the IRS rule that if the basis cannot be established then the basis is zero.

You should do your best to establish the basis in good faith as early as possible. The IRS could challenge the basis during an audit if it is not well defined. You should contact the custodian early and start working on establishing the basis of your RRSPs and other registered accounts before you leave Canada. Obtaining the basis will be more difficult after you leave Canada as dealing with customer service to research this issue can be challenging, and it will be more difficult for you to visit a physical branch.

Establishing the basis of your registered accounts is also important from a federal taxation standpoint. The IRS treats registered accounts in Canada like taxable brokerage accounts in that your original contributions into such accounts come out as a return of capital. This means your contributions are never taxed in the U.S. even though you deducted the income in Canada when you made the contribution and no tax was paid on contributions.

I generally recommend clients liquidate their RRSPs in the year prior to entering the U.S. This is because if you enter the U.S. with nothing but cash in those accounts, the cash balance is your basis. In other words, the basis for cash is its value. This means RRSP distributions can be taken with very little U.S. tax liability in the years immediately following your move to the U.S. The longer you are in the U.S., the more your RRSP distributions will be subject to

U.S. tax, assuming positive investment returns.

The reality is many people do not liquidate their registered accounts to cash before leaving Canada. As you buy and sell securities in the account, you will develop two different cost basis calculations because you are paying tax on income as it comes in at the state level, but only paying tax on part of the distribution at the federal level. You can see how muddy this gets. For practical purposes, what I typically see tax preparers do is establish the basis as a percentage of the account balance on the client's first U.S. tax return, or when they take the first distribution. For example, 50% of the account is taxable. They then report that same percentage of the distribution as taxable in future years until the account is fully distributed.

Theoretically, the percentage that is taxable should go up slightly each year that there are positive market returns, but it is extremely difficult to maintain an accurate basis for these purposes. Some tax laws work better in theory than reality, so good faith should be exercised. Establishing the basis for LIRAs and other types of accounts that result from employer pensions is easy because it is zero. The employee never made any contributions.

When someone moves away from Canada and becomes a resident of another country, they can retain their Canadian citizenship but become a non-resident for tax purposes. This is different from the U.S. in that the U.S. taxes the worldwide income of all its citizens regardless of where they reside. In other words, U.S. citizens must continue to file U.S. tax returns and report their worldwide income no matter where they live. Canadian citizens can stop filing Canadian tax returns once they move away from Canada.

Since U.S. citizens living in Canada must file U.S. tax returns, their IRA distributions are fully taxable on their U.S. tax returns. Canadian citizens living in the U.S. do not file Canadian tax returns, only U.S. returns. Canada imposes a deemed disposition tax when its citizens and residents move away from the country because it allows them to cease tax filing as long as they don't have Canada-sourced income.

There are some exceptions to the deemed disposition tax for what is considered Canadian situs property. This is property that the CRA can attach itself to somehow, and generally includes things like registered retirement accounts and real estate. The withholding rate for registered account distributions is 15% on periodic distributions up to the minimum RRIF amount, double the minimum RRIF amount, or 10% of the account balance at the beginning of the year. All distributions above this amount are considered lump sum and subject to a 25% withholding tax. For this reason, it is usually best to distribute registered funds in amounts that will lead to a 15% withholding.

An exception to this may be if you will be in the U.S. for a limited number of years and then return to Canada. You will be subject to much higher effective tax rates when you return. Your top U.S. tax rate may be 33% if you live in a state like Florida, Nevada or Texas (not including AMT, NIIT or Medicare Surtax). Distributing some of your RRSP as a lump sum may make sense if you move to the U.S. temporarily. This may not make sense for a younger worker because of the time value of money.

Non-resident aliens may also have a withholding tax on their IRA or other qualified distributions. They are not required to file a tax return, but the IRS also wants to make sure they get their taxes. Per the Canada-U.S. Tax Treaty, the withholding rate is 15% for Canadian residents. The withholding rate is 30% for those who move to countries that do not have a tax treaty with the U.S. There are some custodians in the U.S. who will house the IRA or other U.S. retirement accounts of non-residents, although trading may be frozen. You may have to do some research to find a custodian if you want to manage your accounts yourself from abroad.

Only your retirement accounts can be kept in your home country when you move abroad. Your taxable accounts will have to go with you for regulatory reasons. The custodian and investment advisor you work with must be licensed and registered in both the jurisdiction where the client lives, and where the account originated. In a perfect world you could do all the pre-entry planning you need at least a year before you move. This is rarely how things play out.

When I moved from Phoenix to Toronto, I was asked to move at the end of May, and we vacated our home at the end of June to drive to Toronto. I could write a book about all the little things that must be done to prepare for a move like this, from selling a home or breaking a lease, to hiring movers and cleaners, packing, figuring out what to do with the cars, changing addresses, and ordering insurance records, etc. There were so many things to accomplish, and we were able to make it all happen in about a month. To complicate things further, my wife and I had three young children at the time, she was five months pregnant with our youngest, and I was studying for the CFA Level II exam that June. It was a crazy period, which is the case for most working families when they go through a move like this.

Without proper time to prepare, most people will become consumed with the physical move across the border. Most people put their finances on hold during the moving process, so often people do not seek my assistance until after they have already made the move. Others live a cross-border lifestyle, where they live, work, or spend time in both countries, and can be tax residents of both countries. In this case, they will usually use the Treaty Tie Breaker[91] and closer connection[92] rules to determine their country of tax residence. Others have properties in both countries but leave their U.S. address on their taxable account.

Sometimes Canadian residents use a U.S. address for investment accounts

---

[91] https://www.irsstreamlinedprocedures.com/treaty-tiebreaker-tax-rule-closer-connection/

[92] https://www.irs.gov/individuals/international-taxpayers/closer-connection-exception-to-the-substantial-presence-test

for simplicity's sake; other times it is to avoid realizing capital gains. Some do this because they are more familiar with, or prefer, the U.S. market. This can create some tax and regulatory issues because income will be reported to the state where you have the account registered. You should be filing a tax return there to report the income. Also, if you are working with an advisor, they are violating securities regulations by not being licensed and registered in your new home jurisdiction. In general, when you move to another country, your taxable accounts must go with you, which means you may have to realize capital gains in the account.

You may ask, why can't I just transfer the securities I have in the account to a new custodian in my new home country? One reason is because each country has its own stock exchanges. The largest U.S. exchange is the New York Stock Exchange (NYSE). The largest Canadian exchange is the Toronto Stock Exchange (TSX). Most individual stocks and ETFs can be transferred in-kind to your new custodian on the other side of the border, but mutual funds cannot. Custodians can route orders for stocks and ETFs to foreign exchanges, but not orders for mutual funds.

There are really two issues with transferring securities in-kind without selling. The first is whether the security can be held in the new jurisdiction. The second is whether you want to keep the security. We do extensive due diligence to determine which securities we want to include in our models and in what proportions. We have many models based on risk tolerance, citizenship of the client, residency of the client, jurisdiction of the account and currency of the account.

As you can imagine, asset modeling gets very complex. We keep up with the laws, rules, and regulations of both countries. We do continual research on the investment options in both countries and are familiar with the Canada-U.S. Tax Treaty, which dictates how things work when you have assets in both countries. We navigate the tax laws that most domestic advisors do not have to worry about, such as the Passive Foreign Investment Company (PFIC) rules.

You will likely have to make some adjustments to your portfolio when you move across an international border. Embedded capital gains are not a good reason to hold a security long term. At the end of the day, owing capital gains tax is a good thing because it means you made money. You always want to mitigate tax liability when you can, but you do not want to let taxes influence your investment decisions too much, or cause you to be out of compliance. You also do not want to let tax avoidance cause you to stray from your allocation, and hence take on too much risk.

If you are moving from the U.S. to Canada and are not a U.S. citizen or permanent resident, you may want to wait and realize any gains in your U.S. portfolio after you are no longer a U.S. tax resident. You can also do this if you will be renouncing your U.S. citizenship, do not qualify as a covered expatriate, or will not owe any tax because of the significant capital gains exemption given to covered expatriates, which is $866,000 in 2024. You will be required to file IRS Form 8854 in the year of departure, which is when the capital gains calculation takes place.

Only long-term residents can be considered covered expatriates. You are considered a long-term resident if you have been a U.S. citizen or Green Card holder in eight of the previous 15 years. You are a covered expatriate if any of the following statements apply[93]:

- Your average annual net income tax for the five years ending before the date of expatriation or termination of residency is more than a specified amount that is adjusted for inflation, or $201,000 for 2024.
- Your net worth is $2 million or more on the date of your expatriation or termination of residency.
- You fail to certify on Form 8854 that you have complied with all U.S. federal tax obligations for the five years preceding the date of your expatriation or termination of residency.

---

[93] https://www.irs.gov/instructions/i8854

The reason you should wait to sell your holdings until after you are no longer a U.S. tax resident is because no capital gains exemption will be given to you if you sell the securities as a U.S. tax payer. You will not have to report the sale of the securities in the U.S. if it happens after you file your final tax return, including Form 8854, which gives you a $725,000 capital gains exemption on the deemed disposition of those securities. From a Canadian perspective, you get a step-up of the tax cost basis of your assets on your date of entry. If the sale is done shortly after your move to Canada, the capital gains will be minimal.

Following are some of the key differences between the tax systems of Canada and the U.S.:

- In the U.S., married couples can file a joint tax return, called Married Filing Jointly (MFJ), whereas in Canada, each individual files their own tax return. In Canada, some credits are based on household income, and some credits and deductions can be shared between spouses, but they cannot be pooled like when filing a joint return in the U.S.
- In the U.S., separate tax returns are filed with the IRS and the applicable state, while in Canada you file the provincial and federal tax returns together.
- Canada does not tax any gains on the sale of your primary residence. After meeting certain test criteria, the U.S. provides only a $250,000 ($500,000 for married couples) exemption on any gains attributed to the sale of your principal residence. To qualify as a primary residence in the U.S., you must occupy the home for two of the previous five years. In Canada, your primary residence is determined each year. If you have used the property as a rental or vacation home, you may receive a partial capital gains exemption, which is prorated based on the number of years the property was used as your primary residence.

$$\frac{\text{\# of years used as primary residence} + 1}{\text{\# of years owned}}$$

- In Canada, your medical and charitable deductions are calculated as a credit against your tax liability. In the U.S., they are a deduction from taxable income if you itemize deductions.
- In Canada, some deductions that relate to the generation of investment income can be deducted against that income. Unfortunately, any fees paid for investment management are no longer deductible in the U.S.
- In the U.S., you deduct the higher of the basic standard deduction the government gives you or your "itemized" deductions from your income before arriving at your taxable income. There is no longer a personal exemption in the U.S. In Canada, every tax filer gets a personal amount, which can be transferred between spouses if unused.
- Canada includes 50% of the total capital gain in taxable income. The inclusion rate was scheduled to increase to 66.67% for gains above $250,000 in 2025. Justin Trudeau resigned as prime minister in 2025. Mark Carney became the leader of the liberal party and has abandoned the scheduled increase. The conservative party does not support an increase in the capital gains inclusion rate so the measure appears to be dead regardless of which party wins the federal election on April 28, 2025.
- In the U.S., the capital gains rate depends on how long you have held the investment and what your marginal tax bracket is. For investments held for one year or less, the capital gains are taxed as ordinary income just like interest. For investments held for longer than one year, a flat 15% capital gains rate applies for those in the 22%, 24%, 32%, and 35% tax brackets. For those in the 10% or 12% tax brackets, the long-term capital gains rate is 0%. Those in the top tax bracket of 37% pay a long-term capital gains rate of 20%. Note that those in the 35% tax bracket may be split between a 15% and 20% capital gains rate based on their Adjusted Gross Income (AGI). [94]

---

[94] https://www.nerdwallet.com/article/taxes/capital-gains-tax-rates?msockid=26345d234a1d6aec072f49904b996bcc

Capital gains tax rate 2025				
The following rates and brackets apply to long-term capital gains sold in 2025, which are reported on taxes filed in 2026.				
Tax rate	Single	Married filing jointly	Married filing separately	Head of household
0%	$0 to $48,350	$0 to $96,700	$0 to $48,350	$0 to $64,750
15%	$48,351 to $533,400	$96,701 to $600,050	$48,350 to $300,000	$64,751 to $566,700
20%	$533,401 or more	$600,051 or more	$300,001 or more	$566,701 or more
Short-term capital gains are taxed as ordinary income according to federal income tax brackets.				

- Canada allows capital losses to be utilized against capital gains in the current year. Any remaining capital losses can be used against capital gains in the three prior years. Any unutilized losses can be carried forward and applied against future gains. In the U.S., capital losses can also be used to offset capital gains in the current tax year. To the extent that capital losses exceed capital gains, up to $3,000 can be used to reduce other taxable income. Any excess can be carried forward to offset future capital gains, or other income as described above.
- Canada requires a 138% gross-up and ensuing 15.02% federal tax credit on Canadian public company dividends called an eligible dividend. In the U.S., qualified dividends are taxed at a flat 15% tax rate, while non-qualified dividends are taxed at your ordinary marginal income tax rates as high as 37%[95].
- Both countries tax interest as ordinary income subject to your respective marginal tax rate. Canada does not offer tax-free municipal bonds, and U.S. muni bonds are fully taxable for Canadian residents.

---

[95] https://www.taxtips.ca/dtc/eligible-dividend-tax-credit.htm#google_vignette

2025 deductions	Canada (CAD)	U.S. (USD) (MFJ)
Standard deduction/ Spousal amount/personal exemption	16,129 16,129	30,000 15,000
Mortgage interest	X	✓
Property taxes	X	✓
Auto registration	X	✓
Provincial/state or sales taxes	X	X
Medical expenses	3% threshold	7.5% threshold
Charitable contributions	75% of income	60% of income
Contributions to political parties	✓	X
Safe deposit box	X	✓
Tuition and education	✓	✓

2025 credits	Canada (CAD)	U.S. (USD) (MFJ)
Child tax credit	X	2,000 per child
Foreign tax credit	X	X

Tax Form	Canada	U.S.
Personal TaxReturn	T-1	1040
Amended Personal Return	T1-ADJ	1040X
Capital Gains/Losses	Schedule 3	Schedule D
Dividends/Interest	Investment Income and Carrying Charges (previously Schedule 4)	Sche duleB
Charitable Donations	Schdule 9	Schedule A
Corporate Tax Return	T-2	1120
Partnership Tax Return	T5013	1065 or K-1
Trust Tax Return	T-3	1041

7

Moving to the U.S.

Nearly all Americans have ancestors who braved the oceans–liberty-loving risk takers in search of an ideal–the largest voluntary migrations in recorded history. Immigration is not just a link to America's past; it's also a bridge to America's future.

–George W. Bush

Moving permanently to the U.S. does not require you to relinquish your Canadian citizenship. In 1977, Pierre Trudeau announced his "once a Canadian, always a Canadian" policy, which means you will retain your Canadian citizenship even if you leave Canada or become a citizen of another country. Citizens of Canada are not subject to tax on their worldwide income based on citizenship, so there is rarely a compelling reason to renounce Canadian citizenship. Your Canadian citizenship will allow you to return to Canada permanently with no immigration complications should you decide to move back.

Your circumstances will determine whether you are a resident of Canada or the U.S. To cease Canadian residency, your move away from Canada must be permanent in nature. Administratively, the CRA has indicated that if you are absent from Canada for two years or longer, you will be presumed to have become a non-resident if you have severed your residential ties with Canada and established residential ties in another country. The two-year rule does not, however, have strong support in law. Establishing residency, developing social and economic ties, and paying income taxes in any tax treaty-bearing country is helpful in establishing your case.

The courts have held that everyone must be a resident somewhere, and that an individual can be a resident in more than one place at the same time for income tax purposes. Therefore, when a resident of Canada goes abroad, but does not establish a permanent residence elsewhere, there is a presumption that they remain a resident of Canada. When you return to Canada, it is possible that the CRA may require you to provide evidence of residency in the U.S. for tax purposes, such as copies of U.S. tax returns and other documentation proving your physical residency. Also, establishing permanent residence abroad does not, in and of itself, mean that you have become a non-resident of Canada.

In some cases, it may make sense to delay your move across the border based on your income patterns. You will be considered to have a closer connection to a foreign country than to the U.S. if you or the IRS establishes that you have maintained more significant contacts with the foreign country than with the U.S. The Treaty has a series of tie-breaker tests in place that determine tax residency in situations where an individual might be a tax resident of both countries. You can use the Treaty Tie Breaker Rules to maintain residency until it is more advantageous to make the move, but careful planning is required.

The IRS, or the CRA, may challenge your residency status if it is not clear. A U.S. citizen or resident can request assistance from the U.S. competent authority when the actions of Canada, the U.S., or both, potentially result in double taxation or taxation contrary to the Treaty. The U.S. competent authority may then consult with the Canadian competent authority to determine if the double taxation or denial of treaty benefits in question can be avoided. If the competent authorities are not able to reach agreement in a case, binding arbitration proceedings may apply.[96]

At the time you move to the U.S. permanently, it is in your best interest to sever your tax ties with Canada so that you are a tax resident of only one country, which will simplify your life. The CRA does not look at just one item in determining residency but rather a pattern or group of factors to decide if you have sufficiently moved your community of interest out of Canada and established it in the U.S.

The following are among the factors to be considered in making this determination[97]:

---

[96] https://www.irs.gov/pub/irs-pdf/p597.pdf

[97] https://www.canada.ca/en/revenue-agency/services/tax/technical-information/income-tax/income-tax-folios-index/series-5-international-residency/folio-1-residency/income-tax-folio-s5-f1-c1-determining-individual-s-residence-status.html

- Do you have a permanent home available to you in Canada?
- Where are your social and personal ties (church, social clubs, professional organizations, etc.)?
- Where are your economic ties (employment, bank accounts, driver's license, personal property, etc.)?
- Have you established residential ties to another country and are you resident in that country for tax purposes?
- Do you intend to return to Canada later?

You should do the following as soon as possible when you leave Canada:

- When you have secured medical insurance in the U.S., mail your provincial health card back to the authorities of your home province and inform them in writing that you have left for the U.S. and are no longer a resident of Canada.
- Apply for a state driver's license as soon as possible in your new home state. Mail your provincial driver's license back to its issuer along with a letter informing them that you have left for the U.S. and are no longer a resident of Canada.
- Cancel all memberships with any churches, clubs, professional associations, etc. Inform them in writing that you are relocating to the U.S. permanently. You can retain membership of any professional organization on the basis that you are required to perform duties abroad without significantly impacting non-residency status. However, you should arrange for the membership status to be designated "non-resident" if possible. Establish these relationships in the U.S. as applicable.
- Cancel all magazine, newspaper, and media subscriptions.
- Terminate any safety deposit boxes and open a new one in the U.S.
- Move as many of your business and professional relationships to the U.S. as possible. For example, purchase an auto insurance policy in the U.S., establish banking and investment relationships in the U.S., and establish a U.S. estate plan with a U.S. attorney.
- After a year or so of living in the U.S., ensure that you clearly spend more

time in the U.S. than in Canada.

- Take as much of your valuable personal property, collectibles, etc. with you when you cross into the U.S. or shortly thereafter. Sell, donate, or dispose of as many personal possessions not accompanying you abroad. Try not to store many of these items in Canada for any extended period, because the maintenance of personal property in Canada may be an indication that residency was not terminated.

- Consolidate your bank accounts by closing all unnecessary accounts and transferring all or a substantial portion of your funds to a bank account in the U.S. Once you are established in the U.S. and all cheques have cleared against the Canadian accounts, transfer the balance and close all Canadian accounts except those used for convenience and business purposes.

- I usually recommend you cancel all credit cards with Canadian financial institutions that cannot convert your account to a U.S. account. Leaving credit cards open is a tax tie and creates an unnecessary opportunity for identity theft.

- Submit a formal address change to Canada Post to have your mail forwarded to your U.S. address. Notify your contacts that you have a new address in the U.S.

- Establish and maintain a personal file outlining your efforts to cease residency in Canada. The determination of residency status is not straightforward. Although you may have a strong fact pattern, the CRA can assert that individual facts and circumstances do not support the claim that you have ceased residency from Canada. A personal file containing your relevant information may be vital in demonstrating to the CRA that you have sufficiently severed your ties with Canada.

CRA Form NR73 – *Determination of Residency Status* is the form used to establish residency status[98]. You can review this form online to determine if anything else applies to your situation in severing your ties with Canada. I do not recommend you submit this form to the CRA voluntarily, unless

---

[98] https://www.canada.ca/en/revenue-agency/services/forms-publications/forms/nr73.html

requested to do so and proper counsel is sought beforehand, because this form is intentionally tricky. Once submitted and rejected, it can be difficult to change your filing position in Canada.

A common reason to use Form NR73 is to get an official determination of non-residency so you can unlock locked-in retirement accounts. Each province has its own rules for unlocking, so check with your custodian or investment advisor. Several provinces will allow you to roll your locked-in account into your RRSP tax-free. Ontario will let you unlock your account, but you can only take a taxable cash distribution (25% withholding for non-residents). Ontario does not allow you to roll your LIRA into your RRSP.

When you exit Canada, immediately notify all Canadian banks, trust companies, brokerage firms, life insurance companies, mutual fund companies and any other financial institutions with which you have an account in writing. In your letter, provide them with your new address and inform them that you are now non-residents of Canada, subject to the non-resident withholding tax as determined by the Income Tax Act. Currently, there is no withholding on non-RRSP interest, 15% on dividends and pensions, and 0% on CPP/OAS. Per the Canada Income Tax Act, there is a default 25% withholding on lump-sum LIRA and RRSP withdrawals. Be sure to keep copies of your letters as proof of notification in the event these institutions do not withhold the correct amounts.

To sever your ties with Canada and establish yourself as a U.S. resident, you must report to the CRA that you have left Canada. For the year in which you exit Canada, you must file a Canadian "exit return" and report your income and deductions attributable to Canada prior to your departure. Your exit return will not need to be filed until April 30th of the year after your exit. This will be the final personal tax return filed with the CRA unless you re-establish Canadian residency in the future or have Canada-sourced income that is not subject to withholding.

Upon departure from Canada, Canadian residents are considered to have disposed of most property for deemed proceeds equal to the fair market value of the property at that time. If the fair market value of the property exceeds its cost base for income tax purposes, the individual must recognize a capital gain that is taxable in Canada on their final Canadian exit tax return. The three largest deterrents to moving to the U.S. are the deemed disposition tax, currency exchange, and healthcare for those who do not qualify for Medicare.

Married U.S. taxpayers essentially get income splitting by default through filing joint tax returns. In Canada, everyone files their own tax return and careful planning should be done to mitigate joint tax liability. You file a joint return in the U.S., so it does not matter who makes the money or whose name your assets are in; it is all taxed the same during your lifetime. Holding assets jointly is usually better in the U.S. for estate planning purposes. Assets held jointly by married couples do not have to go through probate.

There are a few discrepancies in the way certain income items are handled which seem to favor U.S. citizens or U.S. residents. For example, when you move to the U.S. you will no longer file Canadian tax returns. The "OAS clawback" tax is based on your income so there is no more clawback once you stop filing Canadian tax returns. In 2025, the OAS clawback is triggered when taxable income reaches $90,997 or higher. The reduction in benefits is 15 cents for every dollar above the threshold until benefits are phased out at $148,451.[99]

Taking registered account distributions as a U.S. resident can be much more advantageous than taking distributions as a Canadian resident. As non-residents, your RRSP, RRIF and LIRA distributions are subject to a 15% withholding on periodic payments and a 25% withholding on lump-sum withdrawals. Plus, your distributions are not subject to any provincial income

---

[99] https://www.canada.ca/en/services/benefits/publicpensions/cpp/old-age-security/recovery-tax.html

tax. They could be subject to state income tax, but that depends on which state you live in.

One factor that favors retiring in the U.S. is that IRA distributions are fully taxable for Canadian residents, but RRSP and RRIF distributions are not fully taxable in the U.S. The best strategy to minimize RRSP income in the U.S. is to lock in your basis before you leave Canada. From the perspective of the IRS, if you enter the U.S. holding nothing but cash in your RRSP, that is your basis. Accordingly, you should sell all the securities in your RRSP prior to becoming a U.S. tax resident, so your basis in the RRSP from a U.S. perspective is the value of the account on the day you became a tax resident. This will also alleviate the necessity of having to research the U.S. basis of the account. Yes, you could have some opportunity cost from not being invested for a period, but the tax savings can be huge for those who have been contributing to their RRSP for many years.

For couples moving to the U.S. where one spouse is a U.S. citizen, planning must be done to ensure you liquidate your RRSP prior to becoming a U.S. tax resident because it is best for many couples to take the 6013(g) election on their first joint U.S. tax return. The 6013(g) election allows you to file a complete- year joint return in the year the non-resident spouse becomes a U.S. resident. This gives you access to the joint tax brackets as well as the joint standard deduction. Without the election, each spouse must file a Married Filing Separately (MFS) tax return and itemize deductions. The standard deduction in 2025 is $30,000.

Many couples do not have many itemized deductions in their year of entry unless they purchase a home or have a medical emergency. The Married Filing Jointly tax bracket income thresholds are double those of MFS, so taking the election can result in significant tax savings. All sales within your RRSP should be done at the end of the year prior to establishing U.S. residency. This is because you may become a U.S. resident on January 1st rather than the day you enter the country, because of the election. Your statement on January 1st should show nothing but cash.

Once you lock in your RRSP basis, distributions can be done with minimal tax consequence immediately after your move to the U.S. If you distribute your entire RRSP the day after you sever tax ties with Canada and change your address with the custodian, you will have a 25% withholding tax in Canada and zero tax liability in the U.S. Assuming positive markets, the U.S. tax liability in your RRSP will grow the longer you are a U.S. resident.

If you will remain a U.S. tax resident for the remainder of your life, you should defer the income for as long as possible. If you plan to move back to Canada at some point in the future, and you expect to be in a higher tax bracket in Canada, you should consider taking RRSP distributions while in the U.S. Even if you were only going to be in the U.S. for one year and took the distribution with a 25% withholding, it could save you significant tax liability over time. Also, any money you distribute out of your RRSP at lower tax rates while you are in the U.S. will not be subject to Canadian income tax when the account is deemed disposed of upon your death. If you are a U.S. tax resident when you pass away, your RRSP can be transferred to your spouse, or there will be a 25% withholding tax before it is distributed to the named beneficiary.

Arkansas, California, Delaware, Pennsylvania, and South Carolina do not honor the Canada-U.S. Tax Treaty. If you live in those states, your RRSP investment income is taxable at the state level annually. I am not referring to distribution income. I am referring to dividends, interest, and capital gains within the account. This income is not taxable federally and does not have to be reported on your 1040. An adjustment must be made on your state return to add the income. Distributions are not taxable at the state level.

Some states honor the Canada-U.S. Tax Treaty. In those states, RRSP income is deferred until distribution and is taxable to the same extent as on your federal return. Other states do not allow foreign tax credits at all. Some states only allow credit for tax paid to another state or province, not taxes paid to a federal government (the CRA). The problem with that is once you leave Canada you will not pay any provincial tax as there are no provincial withholding taxes upon distribution.

Many Canadians move to the U.S. with a Tax-Free Savings Account. The problem for U.S. citizens and residents is that the TFSA was not included in the Canada-U.S. Tax Treaty and is fully taxable in the U.S., like taxable brokerage accounts. This is not a huge issue but it will complicate your life, because TFSA income is not tracked by the custodian in Canada. You will have to quantify the income manually, convert it to USD on the date of the transaction, and then report it on your U.S. return. For this reason, I recommend people moving to the U.S. close their TFSA before they leave Canada.

My recommendation may be different for U.S. citizens moving to Canada. These people will have to continue to file U.S. returns and their TFSA will be taxable on their U.S. return. Keeping a TFSA for U.S. citizens living in Canada can still be beneficial for those in high tax brackets because you pay more tax in Canada than the U.S. Since the account is tax-free in Canada, you may have enough other passive foreign tax credits to offset the additional U.S. tax from the TFSA. Even if you cannot apply any foreign tax credits to your TFSA income in the U.S., your overall tax rate will decrease compared to investing in a taxable account in Canada. In the TFSA, you may pay 33% on interest income in the U.S., but that is better than 50% or more in combined federal and provincial taxes in Canada.

The TFSA is not the only account that did not make it into the Treaty. The most popular education savings plans from both countries are not included either. Registered Education Savings Plans in Canada and 529 Education Savings Plans in the U.S. are both fully taxable once you move across the border. This means interest, dividends and capital gains will need to be reported on your tax return in your new home country. 529 plan distributions are not taxable in the U.S. if used at a qualifying higher education institution. Many Canadian universities are approved for the use of 529 funds.

To keep things simple, I usually recommend U.S. citizens transfer their 529 account into the name of a trusted family member such as a parent. You may be essentially gifting this person a lot of money, so trust is important. The owner and beneficiary of 529 plans can be changed within limits. The risk is they could close the account and take the money. The owner can also change the beneficiary, so they could make someone who is not your child the beneficiary.

The two alternatives are to keep the account in your own name and pay the income tax in Canada, or close the account and pay ordinary income tax plus a 10% penalty on the earnings. You get a step-up in the tax cost basis when you enter Canada, so the earnings from the time you enter Canada will be taxable. A new change to unused 529 plans is that up to $35,000 can now be transferred to a Roth IRA owned by the beneficiary if the 529 plan has been open for at least 15 years. 529 contributions must be in the 529 account for at least five years to be eligible for tax-free and penalty-free rollover. Remember, 529 beneficiaries can be changed to many family members, including yourself. You don't have to give your kids a gift toward their retirement if the funds were intended for education and you are disappointed they didn't go to college.

If you are retiring with employer stock options, you need to be aware of the difference in the way the options are taxed. In Canada, the difference between the exercise price and the sale price is included in taxable income. There is a 50% deduction available for stock options resulting in the tax liability being like capital gains tax. 50% of capital gain income is taxable; the options get a 50% deduction. This produces general limitation foreign tax credits, not passive foreign tax credits like capital gains would. In the U.S., the difference between the sale price and the exercise price is taxed as a capital gain. As a result, being awarded or exercising U.S. stock options while living in Canada can result in a mismatch of foreign tax credits.

Most stock options are exercised through what is referred to as a "cashless exercise" which is when the owner exercises the option and sells it simultaneously. No money is needed to exercise the option, which is a major reason why this method is so common. In this situation, or if the stock is sold in less than one year, the resulting gain is short term and is taxed at your marginal income tax rate. If the stock is held for more than one year, the gain is long term and is usually taxed at 15%.

Stock options in the U.S. create passive income and require passive foreign tax credits. General limitation foreign tax credits are generated in Canada, so you have a mismatch of foreign tax credits. Taking the credits as a deduction on Schedule A may be your only option to mitigate double taxation.

Many people decide to either sell their home or rent it out upon moving to the U.S. Canada offers a 100% primary residence capital gains exemption if you sell the home. If you sell the property within one tax year after moving out, you will receive the primary residence exemption. Canada has a formula to determine what portion of your capital gain gets the exemption. The reason you get one year to sell the home is because the formula includes an extra year in the numerator. Again, the primary residence capital gains exemption formula is below:

$$\frac{\text{\# of years used as primary residence} + 1}{\text{\# of years owned}}$$

If you purchased and moved into the home in 2000, then moved to the U.S. in 2024, you would have until the end of 2025 to sell the home with no capital gains tax. If you kept the home beyond 2021, a larger fraction of it would be taxable each year.

The U.S. works a little differently in that the maximum capital gains exemption for your primary residence is $500,000 for married joint filers ($250,000 for individuals). For the property to qualify as your primary residence, you only need to have lived in it as your primary residence for two of the past five years. In the example above, the seller will qualify for the capital gains exemption until 2028. If the home is sold within three years of moving out, and the gain is $500,000 USD or less, there will be no capital gains.

If you decide to use the home as a rental property, you will need to hire an agent or property manager to provide the administration of the property. Fortunately, real estate is not subject to the deemed disposition tax upon your exit because it is considered Canadian situs property. Situs just means the place where something exists. Since real estate is immobile, the CRA does not have to worry about you taking the asset out of the country without paying your tax due.

You will need to complete Form NR6 – *Undertaking to File an Income Tax Return by a Non-Resident Receiving Rent From Real or Immovable Property or Receiving a Timber Royalty*, and send it to the CRA for approval before the first rental payment is due each year. Once approved, your agent can withhold 25% of the net rent rather than 25% of the gross rent.[100] This can make a huge difference. If you are collecting $4,000 per month in rent and do not file Form NR6, you or your agent will have to withhold $12,000 throughout the year but no tax return will need to be filed. These taxes are due and payable monthly by the 15th of the month following the rent payment.

The non-resident rental income tax withholding rate is 25% on net rents. If your NR6 is approved, you must file a Section 216(4) tax return to reconcile the tax and report the rent payments and expenses. With expenses, many owners have little to no net rent, or profit, so nothing needs to be remitted to the CRA throughout the year. A Section 216 return needs to be filed annually, but often there is very little balance or refund after expenses and the capital cost allowance.

Generally, you have to send the CRA your Section 216 return within two years from the end of the year that the rental income was paid or credited to you. If

---

[100] https://www.canada.ca/en/revenue-agency/services/forms-publications/forms/nr6.html

you send the CRA Form NR6 for a certain year and the CRA approves it, you must file Form T1159 – *Income Tax Return for Electing under Section 216* for that year, even if you have no tax payable or you are not expecting a refund, on or before June 30th of the following year, and include the income and expenses from all of your Canadian rental properties. If you have rental income from more than one rental property in Canada and make an election under Section 216, all your Canadian rental income and expenses must be reported together in one Section 216 return.

Also, being a long-distance landlord living in another country can create complications. Unless real estate is your profession, I usually recommend against holding rental property in a country where you do not live. If you rent the property and later move back to Canada and into the property, there will be a change of use deemed disposition tax, which could significantly increase the cost of moving home. Everything becomes more difficult when you cross the border.

Likewise, before you are eligible to sell a property in Canada as a non-resident with a reduced withholding rate, you must get approval from the CRA. To do so, you or your agent must file Form T2062 – *Request by a Non-Resident of Canada for a Certificate of Compliance Related to the Disposition of Taxable Canadian Property.* Your agent will need to withhold 25% of the net sales proceeds as tax payment.[101] Property managers and agents often prepare and file Section 216 returns for their clients. The return is straightforward, so many can complete it themselves. Any Canadian tax preparer should have no problem with a single-family residence Section 216 return.

One advantage of saving in an RRSP is the availability of the Home Buyer's Plan (HBP), which is a program that allows you to withdraw from your RRSP to buy or build a qualifying home for yourself or a related person with a disability.

---

[101] https://www.canada.ca/en/revenue-agency/services/forms-publications/forms/t2062.html

The current HBP limit is $60,000. If you withdraw funds from your RRSP and otherwise meet all the HBP conditions, you generally cannot cancel your participation. However, you must cancel your participation if you become a non-resident.

If you become a non-resident after you buy or build a qualifying home, you must choose one of the following options:

- Repay the remaining HBP balance to your RRSP by the earliest of the following dates:
- Before you file your income tax return for the year that you become a non-resident.
- 60 days after you become a non-resident.
- Include the remaining HBP balance as RRSP income on your tax return for the year that you become a non-resident.

Another popular way of saving for a home in Canada is the in the First Home Savings Account (FHSA). Beginning April 1, 2023, Canadians can now deduct up to $8,000 per year in their FHSA up to a lifetime maximum of $40,000. That is $80,000 for a couple purchasing their first home together, and $200,000 or more for a down payment if used in conjunction with the HBP. You cannot live in an owner-occupied property within the past four years to qualify as a first-time purchaser.

FHSA accounts are a cross between a RRSP and a TFSA. Contributions are deductible and distributions are tax-free if used for a qualifying home purchase. Interestingly, you can still use both programs even if you have owned other property within the past four years if you didn't live in it. This may be the case if you rented out your Canadian property while living and working in the U.S. If you rented during your time in the U.S. and it has been more than four years since you left Canada, you can use the HBP and FHSA to purchase a different home when you return to Canada.

It is usually best to leave your RRSP in Canada when you move to the U.S. It often makes sense to take RRSP distributions while you are in the U.S., if you will be returning to Canada in the future, to take advantage of the potentially lower withholding tax rates applied to registered accounts owned by nonresidents. If done correctly, you will not have much U.S. tax liability resulting from distributions from registered Canadian accounts for the first few years you are in the U.S. It is probably best to leave at least $60,000 in your RRSP if you intend on purchasing a property as a qualified first-time homebuyer when you return to Canada as that distribution will be tax-free.

Like RRSPs, FHSAs are also tax-deferred with the IRS for U.S. residents, but not with all states. No deduction is available for nonresidents, so I do not recommend making any contributions to an FHSA while living in the U.S. Distributions to U.S. residents are subject to the same withholding rates and tax treatment as RRSP distributions to U.S. residents.

If you plan on using your FHSA when you return to Canada, be aware that there is a 15-year deadline to purchase a qualifying home in Canada once the account is opened. The account must be closed before December 31st of the 15th anniversary of account opening. There are also age restrictions on FHSAs as they are only available for those between the ages of 18 and 71. They must be closed by the end of the year you turn 71.

If you are unable to make a qualifying purchase before reaching those deadlines, you can either roll your FHSA balance to your RRSP if you have available room or the remaining balance will be taxed as a RRSP distribution. No additional RRSP room is created if you are unable to use the funds before the deadline. Make sure to consider your tax bracket now and in the future, and how the USD cost basis may change over time, if you have a FHSA that you will not be using, and you know you will have to take that taxable income at some point.

Prior to the enactment of Subpart F in 1962, many U.S. taxpayers achieved deferral of U.S. tax on certain kinds of income, such as dividends, interest, rents, and royalties, by earning such income through foreign corporations. In addition, by placing these corporations in low-tax or no-tax jurisdictions, U.S. taxpayers were able to ensure the income was taxed at a very low rate, until it was repatriated to the U.S., significantly reducing their overall tax liability.

Congress determined that this type of deferral was inappropriate and reacted by enacting Subpart F. The Subpart F provisions eliminate deferral of U.S. tax on some categories of foreign income by taxing certain U.S. persons currently on their pro rata share of such income earned by their Controlled Foreign Corporations (CFCs). A CFC is a foreign corporation of which more than 50% of the total combined voting power or value is owned directly, indirectly, or constructively by U.S. shareholders.[102]

Many people moving to the U.S. were previously business owners or self-employed. Canadian-Controlled Private Corporations are a common way for self-employed individuals to defer personal income and reduce their overall tax rate while they are working. CCPCs are a problem once you become a U.S. tax resident because the CCPC is not recognized as a separate entity by the IRS and any business income coming into the corporation is taxable as personal income to you. You are paying corporate tax in Canada, but you need personal foreign tax credits in the U.S. You have a mismatch of foreign tax credits, leading to double taxation. Additionally, distributions from CCPCs are often taken as dividends which produce individual passive foreign tax credits. Again, you have a mismatch of foreign tax credits, adding to the double taxation.

Additionally, CCPCs are considered a CFC by the IRS. Taxation of foreign income earned by CFCs also significantly changed with the passage of the Tax Cuts and Jobs Act of 2017. Certain previously deferred earnings were immediately taxable under the IRC 965 transition tax. Going forward, a new Subpart F tax regime was established for global intangible low-taxed income

---

[102] https://www.irs.gov/irm/part4/irm_04-061-007

(GILTI), and a dividend received deduction for foreign-sourced dividends was enacted.[103]

In general, the U.S. does not tax a foreign corporation if the foreign corporation neither receives U.S.-sourced income nor engages in U.S.-based activities. However, the U.S. does generally tax all income, wherever derived, of U.S. persons. The Subpart F rules treat a U.S. shareholder of a CFC as if they received its proportionate share of certain categories of the corporation's current earnings and profits. The U.S. shareholder is required to report this income currently in the U.S., whether the CFC makes a distribution or not. Subpart F, therefore, does not purport to tax the CFC. Rather, its rules apply only to a U.S. person who owns, directly or indirectly, 10% or more of the voting stock of a foreign corporation that is controlled by U.S. shareholders. The provisions of Subpart F are exceedingly intricate and contain numerous general rules, special rules, definitions, exceptions, exclusions, and limitations, which require careful consideration.

CFC income is reported on Form 5471 – *Information Return of U.S. Persons With Respect to Certain Foreign Corporations.* Form 5471 is used by certain U.S. persons who are officers, directors, or shareholders in certain foreign corporations.[104] The form and schedules are used to satisfy the reporting requirements of sections 6038 and 6046, and the related regulations, as well as to report amounts related to Section 965. Many people want to do their taxes on their own or use a U.S. domestic tax preparer. If you are filing Form 5471, your return is getting pretty complex and you should likely use a Canada-U.S. cross-border tax specialist.

You may have ongoing business and need to maintain the current structure. If

---

[103] https://www.irs.gov/newsroom/tax-cuts-and-jobs-act-a-comparison-for-large-businesses-and-international-taxpayers#:~:text=A%20100%20percent%20deduction%20is,%C2%A7of%20those%20foreign%20corporations

[104] https://www.irs.gov/forms-pubs/about-form-5471

that is the case, you will likely be forced to pay the additional tax. Otherwise, I usually recommend clients close their CCPC prior to departing Canada. If you can change the business structure, you may be able to open an Unlimited Liability Company (ULC) in Canada, which is a pass-through entity. This will cause the corporate income to pass through to you personally, creating personal foreign tax credits that can be used in the U.S. to offset the same income, rather than corporate foreign tax credits which lead to a mismatch of foreign tax credits in the U.S. International business structures are beyond the scope of this book.

The one situation where I have recommended clients keep their CCPC open with money in it is for Medicare purposes. Generally, Medicare is available for people aged 65 or over, younger people with disabilities, and people with end-stage renal disease (permanent kidney failure requiring dialysis or transplant). Medicare has two parts: Part A (hospital insurance) and Part B (doctor's office insurance). You are eligible for premium-free Part A if you are aged 65 or over, you have lived in the U.S. for five years or more, and you or your spouse worked and paid Medicare (FICA) taxes for at least 10 years. Medicare is the cheapest health insurance option in the U.S. for those aged 65 or over, by a significant margin.

The reason you keep the CCPC open if you are moving permanently to the U.S. and do not qualify for Medicare is because you can continue to pay yourself from the CCPC as a U.S. resident. For this to work, your CCPC must remain active and continue to conduct business, although your business activity can decrease compared to when you were in Canada. You cannot just keep funds in the CCPC and take distributions in the U.S. so you can qualify for Medicare. You must continue to have active business earnings.

When you file your 1040 U.S. tax return, you will report the income and pay self-employment tax, which is FICA tax. The self-employment tax rate is 15.3%. The rate consists of two parts: 12.4% for SS and 2.9% for Medicare. For 2025, the first $176,100 of your combined wages, tips, and net earnings is subject to self-employment tax. You can deduct the employer-equivalent portion of your self-employment tax in figuring out your adjusted gross income. Under Section 2042 of the Small Business Jobs Act, a deduction for income tax purposes is allowed to self-employed individuals for the cost of health insurance. This deduction is considered in calculating net earnings from self-employment on Schedule SE. You will be able to deduct your health insurance premiums as a business expense while you wait to become eligible for Medicare.

You become eligible for free Medicare Part A after working 40 eligible quarters. When you work and pay FICA taxes, you earn "credits" toward SS benefits. The number of credits you need to get retirement benefits depends on when you were born. If you were born in 1929 or later, you need 40 quarters (10 years) of work. Once you reach age 62, the Social Security Totalization Agreement with Canada would make you eligible for an SS benefit if you worked in Canada and also paid into the system through FICA taxes, even if not for 10 years. This is because your years worked in Canada help you qualify for a benefit. Your SS benefit will be small and based on your contributions, but you will qualify sooner.

The Totalization Agreement does not affect Medicare eligibility. To qualify for Medicare, you will need to pay FICA taxes for the full 10 years. The amount of earnings it takes to earn a credit may change each year. In 2025, you must earn $1,810 in covered earnings to get one quarter of credit, and $7,240 to get the maximum four credits for the year. This is the minimum amount of business income you will need to generate in your CCPC each year, after deductions, if you want to qualify for Medicare in 10 years. It is important that the CCPC distributions come to you as employment income rather than dividends.

If you move to the U.S. prior to age 65 and are retired or self-employed, you will need to obtain health insurance until you become eligible for Medicare. If everyone in your family is healthy, you may be able to qualify for private short-term insurance. This requires underwriting and you will be turned down if you have pre-existing conditions. Also, since it is short term, it needs to be renewed every six months in most counties. This is the most cost-effective option, but it can be unreliable and insurance carriers have been known to be difficult when it comes to paying claims.

There are also faith-based insurance plans available. Most of these require prescribing to a specific way of living, including restrictions on activities like smoking. The plans charge a monthly premium. You must pay for medical services out of pocket and then file a claim with the plan administrator for reimbursement. This can also be an affordable option but may require more money out of pocket for services and a wait time for reimbursement.

The last health insurance option for those under 65 and without access to an employer provided health insurance plan is through the exchanges established with the Affordable Care Act (ACA). These policies are "guaranteed issue", which means you cannot be denied coverage because of pre-existing conditions. Because it is guaranteed coverage, premiums are quite expensive and vary from county to county. There are also minimum coverage requirements for every plan, which also increases premiums.

ACA-compliant policies are far more expensive than private short-term plans or faith-based plans, but they may be your only option. Fortunately, you can deduct the premiums on Schedule C. Plans are usually available through major carriers like Blue Cross and United Healthcare, so coverage and access are good. Generous premium tax credits are available for ACA-compliant policies.[105] Planning can be done to ensure you qualify for premium tax credits. I have worked with many clients who are millionaires and are receiving free health insurance because of premium tax credits, which are based strictly on MAGI, not net worth.

---

[105] https://www.healthcare.gov/

One important thing to remember is that you are no longer eligible for provincial health coverage once you become a non-resident of Canada. When you travel to Canada to visit, you will need to ensure you have travel insurance. Travel insurance can be long term or short term. Short-term policies are meant to cover you for short trips like vacations. They do not cover doctor's visits or routine services. They are designed for emergencies only and will provide medical coverage abroad until you are well enough to return to your home, where you should have long-term health insurance to cover future treatment.

Long-term travel insurance, which is international health insurance, is meant for those who live an international lifestyle or will be living in a foreign country for an extended period. Policies are usually affordable but do require underwriting and exclude pre-existing conditions. Policies must be renewed annually, and many insurers have age restrictions, meaning they will no longer renew the policy after a certain age. Pricing is done in age brackets, so everyone of the same age who qualifies medically will pay the same premium.

Those who spend several months in Canada, but are not tax residents, should have a long-term insurance policy. These policies work like ordinary health insurance, where they pay either a fixed amount depending on the service provided, or they pay a percentage of the overall cost. Most of these policies are accepted all over the world and provide good coverage. As with any insurance, there have been stories of providers being difficult when it comes to paying claims, which is why it is important to work with a reputable company. I usually recommend working with a broker who can shop several companies.

8

Moving to Canada

"Canada is like a loft
apartment over a really
great party."

– Robin Williams

When you establish tax residency in Canada, you are deemed to have disposed of all your property immediately beforehand, with some exceptions. You are then deemed to have acquired all that property at the same time, at a cost equal to the current fair market value. In effect, at the date of establishing Canadian residency, you are entitled to a "step-up" in the tax basis of your assets. Your future capital gain or loss upon a future sale in Canada, or deemed disposition due to exiting Canada, will be based on the stepped-up value, not the original purchase price. Therefore, it is important to establish fair market values of all property on the date you will be deemed to take up Canadian tax residency.

Some people will cease tax residency with the U.S. when they move to Canada; others will not. Those who are U.S. citizens will remain U.S. tax residents and will have to continue to file U.S. federal tax returns. The U.S. is one of two countries in the world that levies income taxes on worldwide income based on citizenship and residency, rather than just on residency. Eritrea is the other country. Most people do not actually pay much tax in the U.S. once they are Canadian residents because they pay more tax in Canada. The tax paid in Canada can be used as foreign tax credits to offset tax in the U.S. Usually people have enough foreign tax credits to eliminate most or all U.S. tax, with the exception being those who pay the AMT, NIIT, or Medicare Surtax, which may limit the use of foreign tax credits.

Additionally, the U.S. offers the foreign earned income exclusion to reduce double taxation. The exclusion is $130,000 in 2025. If you have foreign earned income, you claim the exclusion by filing Form 2555 – *Foreign Earned Income* with your U.S. tax return.[106] If you claim, and qualify for, the foreign earned income exclusion, you must figure out the tax on your remaining non-excluded income using the tax rates that would have applied had you not claimed the exclusion. In other words, your foreign earned income is not taxable up to the exclusion limit, but the income will be included when

---

[106] https://www.irs.gov/forms-pubs/about-form-2555

figuring out your tax bracket.

Those who are not U.S. citizens will cease U.S. tax residency once they leave. Resident alien visas must be forfeited once you become a non-resident. These include visas such as the TN and L-1. Permanent residents usually surrender their Green Card when they move to Canada, but some do not. You are ineligible for a Green Card as a non-resident so you will lose it eventually whether you surrender it or have it revoked.

If you are considered a covered expatriate, you will be subject to the expatriation tax[107], where your assets will be subject to a "mark-to-market" disposition of your worldwide assets. Covered expatriates are allowed a capital gains exemption of $866,000 USD in 2024. Any gains above this amount will be subject to income tax. IRAs and other U.S. qualified retirement accounts will not be included in the calculation of the expatriation tax. RRSPs and other registered retirement accounts in Canada will be included.

U.S. immigration law holds that a resident alien (Green Card holder) may not stay outside the U.S. for one year without losing his/her legal permanent resident status. If you believe you may be returning to the U.S. within a few years, you can file for a "Reentry Permit"[108]. This is granted to Green Card holders for a two-year period, and allows them to retain their Green Card while being a tax resident of another country. The permit can be renewed a limited number of times, and U.S. tax returns need to be filed while living abroad.

Former Green Card holders who have been out of the U.S. for more than one year and wish to return to the U.S. to live may be eligible for a Returning Resident Visa[109]. This is difficult for most to obtain because you must prove

---

[107] https://www.irs.gov/individuals/international-taxpayers/expatriation-tax

[108] https://www.uscis.gov/sites/default/files/document/guides/B5en.pdf

[109] https://travel.state.gov/content/travel/en/us-visas/immigrate/returning-resident.html

that you remained outside of the U.S. for reasons beyond your control.

Many people who move to Canada and sever tax ties with the U.S. plan on visiting the U.S. in the future. If you are keeping a vacation home in the U.S., or have kids or grandkids remaining there, you need to be aware of the Substantial Presence Test[110]. Even though you have severed tax ties with the U.S., you may be required to file a U.S. tax return if you spend too much time there.

You will be considered a U.S. resident for tax purposes if you meet the Substantial Presence Test's criteria for the calendar year:

- 31 days during the current year; and
- 183 days during the three-year period that includes the current year and the two years immediately before that, counting:
- All the days you were present in the current year, and
- One third1/3 of the days you were present in the first year before the current year, and
- One sixth1/6 of the days you were present in the second year before the current year.

Even if you fail the Substantial Presence Test, you can still be treated as a non-resident alien if you qualify for the closer connection exception available to all aliens.

You qualify for the closer connection exception if you:

- Were present in the U.S. fewer than 183 days during the year; and
- Had a closer connection during the year to one foreign country in which you have a tax home than to the U.S.; and

---

[110] https://www.irs.gov/individuals/international-taxpayers/substantial-presence-test

- Maintained a tax home in that foreign country during the entire year; and
- Had not taken steps toward, and did not have an application pending for, lawful permanent resident status (Green Card).

You will be considered to have a closer connection to a foreign country if you or the IRS establishes that you have maintained more significant contacts with the foreign country than with the U.S. In determining this, considerations include, but are not limited to:

- The country of residence you designate on forms and documents;
- The types of official forms and documents you file;
- The location of:
- Your permanent home,
- Your family,
- Your personal belongings, such as cars, furniture, clothing, and jewelry,
- Your current social, political, cultural, or religious affiliations,
- Your business activities (other than those that constitute your tax home),
- The jurisdiction in which you hold a driver's license,
- The jurisdiction in which you vote,
- Charitable organizations to which you contribute.

You must file Form 8840 – *Closer Connection Exception Statement for Aliens* to claim the Closer Connection Exception[111]. If you are filing a U.S. federal income tax return, attach Form 8840 to it. If you do not have to file a U.S. federal income tax return, send Form 8840 to the IRS by the due date for filing the income tax return.[112]

Many U.S. citizens who no longer live in the U.S. contemplate giving up their

---

[111] https://www.irs.gov/individuals/international-taxpayers/closer-connection-exception-to-the-substantial-presence-test

[112] https://www.irs.gov/forms-pubs/about-form-8840

U.S. citizenship to escape U.S. income and estate taxes[113]. Sometimes Canadian advisors suggest Americans give up their citizenship. It is not easy to renounce your citizenship for the purposes of avoiding tax liability, or the ongoing tax filing obligation. Unless you have other non-tax related reasons to do so, I generally recommend against renouncing your U.S. citizenship. You will have the inconvenience and added expense of filing U.S. tax returns for the rest of your life, but this does not result in any additional tax paid for most people because of foreign tax credits and the foreign earned income exclusion.

It is important to satisfy all foreign asset reporting requirements to avoid unnecessary fines and penalties.[114] These forms include:

- United States Financial Crimes Enforcement Network (FinCEN) Form 114 – *Report of Foreign Bank and Financial Accounts* (FBAR). This form reports your accounts located outside of the U.S. where the combined assets are in excess of $10,000 USD at any time during the year.
- The FBAR is due at the same time you file your U.S. tax return, or April 15th in most years. Your FBAR deadline is automatically extended if you file an extension on your tax return.
- IRS Form 8938 – *Statement of Specified Foreign Financial Assets.* This is due with your income tax return, including any applicable extensions. For taxpayers living within the U.S., reporting is required where the total value of foreign assets was greater than $100,000 USD on December 31st or greater than $150,000 USD at any time during the year (joint tax filers). Those limits go up to $600,000 at any time of the year, or $400,000 on the last day or the year for non-resident joint filers.

Since you are not a Canadian tax resident until you cross the border, you should do your tax planning before you become a tax resident. The CRA does not know anything about you until you start filing tax returns in Canada. You

---

[113] https://www.usa.gov/renounce-lose-citizenship

[114] https://www.irs.gov/businesses/comparison-of-form-8938-and-fbar-requirements

may have filed Canadian tax returns before moving to the U.S., but that is the last record the CRA has of you. It does not know what your income or assets are, your spouse or partner's income or assets, or the ownership structure of your combined assets prior to your tax residency date. This gives you the opportunity to arrange your assets in the way that is most advantageous for you as Canadian taxpayers prior to revealing your financial situation to the CRA. Often this involves gifting taxable investment accounts and income-producing assets into the name of the lower-income spouse. Be aware of the gifting rules in the U.S. and consider estate implications if there are age or life expectancy differences between spouses.

All gifting must be done before becoming Canadian residents or Canada's Income Attribution Rules[115] will apply and negate any tax benefit. The Income Attribution Rules state that when someone transfers or loans property (including money) to their spouse, or to a trust in which that spouse has a beneficial interest, any income or loss from the property is attributed to the spouse who gave the gift and must be included in their income for tax purposes. Income attribution can also apply to gifts to children, grandchildren, parents, and others whom you do not deal with at arm's length.

Married couples should view their combined assets as one portfolio. A joint risk tolerance should be determined which will determine the portfolio's mix of stocks and bonds. In a cross-border context, asset placement also applies between spouses. If you are unable to rearrange the ownership of your assets before you leave, or if one spouse is in a higher tax bracket than the other and you both have taxable investment accounts, it may be best to put interest-producing securities in the name of the spouse in the lower tax bracket. Both dividends and capital gains get preferred tax treatment in Canada as well, so it is best if the spouse in the higher tax bracket holds the equity securities.

---

[115] https://www.canada.ca/en/revenue-agency/services/forms-publications/publications/it511 r/archived-interspousal-certain-other-transfers-loans-property.html

You should also consider which accounts you are saving in prior to retirement. For most people, it is best to save in your 401(k) as much as possible so you can reduce your taxable income and then take the income in retirement when you have less income. Even though you may have less income in retirement, you may still be in a higher tax bracket if you are retiring to Canada. For example, if you are in the 22% federal tax bracket in the U.S. while you are working, you likely expect to be in the 12% tax bracket when you retire. In Ontario, the bottom combined income tax rate is 20.05%. Many U.S. retirees will find themselves paying 30% or more. In this case, it is best to save in a Roth IRA rather than your deductible 401(k).

Many employers offer a Roth 401(k) option. This is ideal in this situation because a Roth 401(k) has the same contribution limit as a deductible 401(k), which is much larger than a Roth IRA ($23,500[116] vs. $7,000[117]). You will pay tax now at 12% or 22% but avoid tax later at 30% or more. You will also reduce your future RMDs and have tax-free retirement income in retirement. If you have flexibility in your move date, it may be best for you to wait and move a year or two after you retire. This way, you can do a Roth conversion the year you leave the U.S., but before you become Canadian residents.

Carrying assets in different currencies or investing in a currency other than that which you will ultimately need to live on introduces currency exchange risk to your situation. I believe in reducing risk as much as possible and recommend you hold Canadian dollars (CAD) when possible. Because you will need CAD to fund your future lifestyle, I recommend migrating these funds opportunistically to CAD when exchange rates are favorable and before you need the money.

---

[116] https://www.irs.gov/newsroom/401k-limit-increases-to-23500-for-2025-ira-limit-remains-7000

[117] https://www.irs.gov/retirement-plans/plan-participant-employee/retirement-topics-ira-contribution-limits#:~:text=For%202020%20and%202019%2C%20the,taxable%20compensation%20for%20the%20year

Often there are capital gains in your taxable U.S. dollar (USD) account that would have to be realized if funds were converted. Also, there are more investment options in USD accounts than CAD. An argument can be made that it is better to invest in USD, but we don't know which stock market or currency will do better over your investment period. Control what you can and convert to the currency you will need, and try to do so when it is advantageous.

The Canada Income Tax Act allows for an equivalent increase in RRSP room in any calendar year that a Canadian tax resident makes a voluntary IRA distribution that is not an RMD. For example, if you were to distribute an IRA of $400,000 USD, you would automatically be eligible to make an RRSP contribution of $500,000 CAD (exchange rate of 1.25). The distribution is fully taxable in both countries for U.S. tax residents. For those who are no longer U.S. tax residents and are now residents of Canada, there would be a 15% withholding tax of $60,000 USD.

You would have to deposit some of your taxable funds to take full advantage of the increased RRSP room. U.S. custodians often withhold the incorrect amount of 30%. You must then file a 1040NR to reconcile your U.S. tax obligation and request the additional 15% as a refund from the IRS. Both RRSPs and IRAs are fully taxable when distributed to Canadian residents. While this is an option, it can be complex to execute and there is rarely a tax advantage.[118] In fact, the tax paid in the U.S. is lost capital and will result in lower investment income in the future.

Situations where this may make sense for the beneficiary are if they are young and their income is low, or if they inherit a large IRA and decide to retire early. In both cases, it makes sense to deposit the funds into an RRSP as they are in low tax brackets and Inherited IRAs require immediate RMDs and the account must be fully distributed within 10 years. This would not make sense

---

[118] https://www.investmentexecutive.com/inside-track_/jamie-golombek/ira-to-rrsp-transfers-can-be-done-but-be-careful/

for someone close to age 72, but it is advantageous for younger people because of the amount of years they have for investment income deferral.

Some people may retire to Canada after working their entire career in the U.S. and saving diligently in their 401(k). This may lead some married couples to have significant IRA balances. If they retire before age 72, it may make sense for them to take early IRA distributions. They should not do Roth conversions as Canadian residents, but they may still want to take some distributions early in retirement at lower tax rates before they are pushed into higher tax rates later in retirement. People in this situation may be pushed into the top tax brackets because of RMDs, especially when the U.S. dollar is strong.

I have had requests to look for ways to move more money out of both Canada and the U.S. Some people feel that the government in either country is running the country into the ground and that they want to get their money out. Those requests have happened for different reasons throughout my career, usually depending on which political party is in power and which way the client leans politically.

A nice tax benefit still available to Canadian residents is deductibility of investment management fees. Any fees paid for managing your money are tax deductible as carrying charges on your Canadian return. For U.S. purposes, all these same fees were previously deductible as itemized deductions and were eliminated with the passing of the Tax Cuts and Jobs Act of 2017[119].

There are some differences between the way accounts are taxed in Canada and the U.S. The IRA and the RRSP are equivalents in their respective countries. The contribution and RMD amounts are different, but they function in the same way. Despite that, the U.S. taxes RRSPs differently than Canada taxes IRAs.

---

[119] https://money.usnews.com/money/personal-finance/taxes/articles/tax-deductions-that-disappeared-this-year

IRAs are simple: they are fully taxable when distributed in both countries. RRSPs are more confusing because distributions are fully taxable for Canadian residents, but the IRS only taxes the growth on the account. All contributions can be distributed tax-free, even though the contributions were made pre-tax. In this respect, it is more tax efficient to retire in the U.S. Also, the IRA withholding amount is 15% for Canadian residents regardless of the distribution amount, while registered account distributions have a withholding rate of 15% or 25% for U.S. residents depending on how much is being distributed.

Those of you who are charitably inclined should consider making your donations out of your IRA through a qualified charitable donation (QCD). Once you reach age 70½, you are eligible to make tax-free IRA distributions of up to $100,000 per year, paid directly from your IRA to the charity of your choice through a QCD. This will benefit both you and the recipient because:

- It reduces your tax liability because you never have to pay income tax on the IRA distribution (rather than distributing the funds to yourself and then making the donation from your chequing account).
- The church or charity may receive more donations because donors have more money available to give because they are not paying income taxes on their money before they donate.

Unfortunately, all IRA distributions are taxable in Canada, even if the funds go directly to a qualified charity. It is possible to get tax credits for charitable donations, but the income itself will be taxable. All QCDs should be done before you become Canadian tax residents.

You can likely expect investing to be more expensive when you move to Canada. Canada has been criticized by the World Trade Organization for the high cost of investing there. Expense ratios on Canadian mutual funds are commonly as high as 2% to 3%, although they have started to decrease in recent years. To put this in perspective, expense ratios on ETFs usually range from 0.03%

to 0.5%. U.S. retail mutual fund expense ratios generally range from 0.5% to 1.25%. Institutional class funds usually have expense ratios of less than 0.5%.

To put it simply, it is very expensive to invest in Canada. As an investment manager in Canada, I focus on minimizing expenses and improving tax efficiency. Our investment portfolios focus on low-cost ETFs and mutual funds, and the expense ratios on the funds we use in Canada are comparable to those funds we use in the U.S., although there are not as many options. Minimizing expenses and being tax efficient helps to maximize your return on investment.

9

Government Retirement Pensions

The trouble with retirement is that you never get a day off.

– Abe Lemons

In Canada, 100% of your Canada Pension Plan and Old Age Security benefits are taxable when received. In the U.S., 85% of your SS benefits are taxable for most people, based on income. Because of the Social Security Totalization Agreement, your government retirement pension benefits are only taxable in your country of residence. Once in Canada, U.S. citizens no longer have to report their SS income on their U.S. tax return, but it is fully taxable in Canada.

Likewise, when you move to the U.S., there is no withholding on your CPP and OAS benefits in Canada, and those benefits are reported on your U.S. 1040 tax return like SS benefits. This means you get 15% of your CPP and OAS benefits tax-free, just like with SS. CPP and OAS benefits are 100% taxable for Canadian residents and 85% taxable for U.S. residents. Canadian residents receive a 15% deduction on SS benefits only, so those benefits are taxed like they are in the U.S. If you sever your tax ties with the U.S., your immigration and tax status will not affect the benefits you have earned through SS and Medicare.

The maximum SS benefit is significantly larger than the maximum CPP or OAS benefits. Here is a 2025 snapshot of the maximum benefit for each pension for those filing at age 70:

- SS – $4,982 USD ($6,228 CAD)[120]
- CPP – $2,035 CAD ($1,628 USD)[121]
- OAS – $990 CAD ($792 USD)[122]

If you want to take a government pension before age 70 and you live in Canada, taking Social Security first may seem logical because of the 15% tax deduction. That may make sense for some, but it depends on how much you expect

---

[120] https://www.ssa.gov/news/press/factsheets/colafacts2025.pdf?ftag=YHF4eb9d17

[121] https://www.canada.ca/en/services/benefits/publicpensions/cpp/cpp-benefit/amount.html

[122] https://www.canada.ca/en/services/benefits/publicpensions/cpp/old-age-security/payments.html

to get from each pension, SS, CPP, and OAS. In other words, depending on how long you worked in the U.S., your taxable SS benefit may be larger than your combined CPP and OAS benefits. The maximum combined CPP and OAS benefit is currently only about 30% of the maximum SS benefit. In that case, you should likely choose to take one of your smaller pensions early. Keep in mind that CPP rewards you the most for waiting (8.4%), followed by SS (8%), then OAS (7.2%).

For those who do not qualify for an SS benefit through U.S. work credits, or OAS because of minimum residency requirements in Canada, the Social Security Totalization Agreement will enable you to receive a benefit. Your years worked in Canada will help you reach the 40 quarters necessary to qualify for an SS benefit. The income you earn in Canada will not be included in the calculation of your benefit as it will be based on your U.S. contributions only.

Likewise, if you have not lived in Canada for the 10-plus years necessary to qualify for an OAS benefit, your years lived in the U.S. will allow you to qualify. Your years lived in the U.S. will not count towards your benefit as it will be based on your Canadian residency only. The ratio used to calculate your OAS benefit (x/40) will increase each year you live in Canada, resulting in a progressively larger benefit each year until you are earning the maximum benefit. Your OAS payment ratio stops increasing when you initiate receipt of your benefit, or at age 70. The Totalization Agreement has nothing to do with CPP benefits, as those are based on contributions into the system only. There is no minimum work history or contribution amount.

As mentioned earlier, all government retirement pension benefits can be maximized by waiting until age 70 to take benefits. This may result in lower gross benefits than taking them early at age 60 (62 for SS) if you die before about age 80. This decision involves a gamble on how long you are going to live. There are two ways to hedge your bets: either take your benefits sometime before 70, or take some benefits early and some late. For example, you could take SS at 62, OAS at 65 and CPP at 70; or you could take them all at 67 if you feel you will live until around 77. I usually recommend you take them either early or late, not at FRA. Every person must decide for themselves based on their own circumstances and intuition.

Married couples can hedge their bets by taking one or two benefits early and one or two benefits late. You need to quantify your potential benefits before you make this decision. We will assume SS is the largest benefit coming to both spouses. In this case, some couples may decide to wait on SS and take other retirement benefits early. The rationale is that they want to get the most out of their largest benefit later in life, but that the other pensions will help take pressure off their portfolio in the early retirement years. It will also ensure they get some government benefits if they pass away prematurely.

Others may decide they want to get what they can out of SS in case they pass away prematurely by taking benefits at 62. The penalty for taking SS early is lower than for CPP (6% vs. 7.2%), so mathematically it is better to take SS early than it is to take CPP early. With SS being your largest benefit, it is better to initiate receipt at age 70 if you live into your mid-80s. The breakeven age will vary depending on actual benefit amounts.

Other couples will make this decision based on the age of each spouse and their benefit amount. As discussed earlier, the decision on when to take SS changes drastically when spousal benefits are involved. This is because receipt of spousal benefits cannot begin until the insured spouse begins to take their benefit, and spousal benefits do not continue to grow after FRA.

Here are the considerations you should make when deciding when to take each spouse's benefit:

1. First, quantify each spouse's benefits.
2. Wait until age 70 if you think you will live past age 80.
3. Take benefits as early as possible if you think you will die before 80.
4. If spousal SS benefits are involved, you should likely take benefits when

the insured spouse is 70 or when the non-insured spouse reaches FRA, whichever comes first. The non-insured spouse can wait until FRA if the insured spouse reaches 70 first.

5. Remember spousal benefits and survivor benefits are both adjusted based on when the receiving spouse originally took their SS benefits.

6. Knowing that Canadian CPP survivor's benefits are cumulative, whereas SS survivor's benefits are based on the deceased spouse's benefit, may factor into your decision on when to take benefits.

7. The age difference between spouses should be considered when deciding distribution order with government retirement pensions as well as with distributions from your retirement and investment accounts.

8. Remember the penalty for taking SS early is lower than for CPP, and the benefit for taking CPP late is greater than for SS.

9. Consider your overall tax planning. You should wait if you are doing Roth conversions or taking early distributions for tax purposes. Taking government pensions at this time will only push you into higher tax brackets or limit your distributions.

10. The OAS clawback should be considered for those in Canada. For example, if you are doing early distributions as a Canadian resident and your income will cause your OAS to be clawed back, there is no point in taking benefits before 70 as they will likely be clawed back anyway. For some, the only way to get OAS is to do a good job of tax planning by delaying pensions and getting funds out of tax-deferred accounts early in retirement.

11. Medicare Part B premiums are based on income and should be considered when doing tax planning.

12. Obamacare premium credits should be considered for U.S. residents who are younger than 65 or do not qualify for Medicare.

10

Estate Planning

When a man retires and time is no longer a matter of urgent importance, his colleagues generally present him with a watch."
— R. C. Sherriff

What is estate planning? The purpose of estate planning is to:

- Control your property while you are alive;
- Take care of you and your loved ones financially if you become disabled;
- Provide instructions for your care if you become disabled;
- Give what you own to whom you want, how you want, and when you want;
- Provide instructions for passing on your *values* (religion, education, hard work, etc.) in addition to your valuables;
- Name a guardian and an inheritance manager for minor children;
- Provide for family members with special needs without disrupting government benefits;
- Provide for loved ones who might be irresponsible with money or who may need future protection from creditors or divorce;
- Provide for the transfer of your business at your retirement, disability, or death;
- Minimize taxes, court costs, and unnecessary legal fees.

Estate planning[123] should be an ongoing process, not a one-time event. Your plan should be reviewed and updated as your family and financial situations (and laws) change over your lifetime.

The four documents that typically make up a U.S. estate plan are:

Revocable Living Trust – A Revocable Living Trust (RLT) is a trust document created by an individual that can be changed over time. RLTs are used to avoid probate and to protect the privacy of the trust owner and beneficiaries of the trust, as well as minimize estate taxes. Revocable trusts, however, have several limitations, including the expense of having them written up, and they lack some of the features of an irrevocable trust.[124]

---

[123] https://www.estateplanning.com/What-is-Estate-Planning/

[124] https://www.irs.gov/pub/irs-tege/eotopicf01.pdf

Overall, a living trust[125] offers you the following benefits:

- It allows you to avoid the probate process with its attendant costs and delays.
- It allows you as much, or as little, control as possible over your estate in a variety of circumstances.
- Your estate will be kept private and will not be a matter of public record for all to see.
- There is less opportunity to contest the provisions of a trust compared to a will.
- It eliminates the need for a court hearing to determine who is to administer your estate in the event of your death or incapacity.
- It alleviates the burden on your heirs to make difficult decisions about your money during an emotional time.

Last Will – A last will and testament is a legal document that communicates a person's final wishes pertaining to assets and dependents. It outlines what to do with a person's possessions, whether the deceased will leave them to another person, a group, or donate them to charity, and what happens to other things he or she is responsible for, such as custody of dependents, and management of accounts and interests. Some states do allow for unusual wills, such as a holographic will[126], which is a handwritten will that is not prepared by an attorney. Different states have various requirements for them to be valid.

General Durable Power of Attorney – While a conventional power of attorney (POA) lapses when the creator of a will becomes mentally incapacitated, a "durable power of attorney" (DPOA) remains in force to enable the agent to manage the creator's affairs and control certain legal, property, or financial matters specifically spelled out in the agreement . A "springing POA" comes

---

[125] https://www.investopedia.com/articles/pf/06/revocablelivingtrust.asp

[126] https://www.investopedia.com/terms/l/last-will-and-testament.asp

into effect only if the creator of the POA becomes incapacitated. A general power of attorney acts on behalf of the "principal" (the will creator) in all matters, as allowed by the state. The agent under a general POA agreement may be authorized to take care of issues such as handling bank accounts, signing cheques, selling property and assets like stocks, and filing taxes. While a DPOA can pay medical bills on behalf of the principal, the durable agent cannot make decisions related to the principal's health.[127] For example, taking the principal off life support is not up to a DPOA.

Healthcare Directives – Living wills and other advance directives are written legal instructions regarding your preferences for medical care if you are unable to make decisions for yourself. Advance directives guide choices for doctors and caregivers if you are terminally ill, seriously injured, in a coma, in the late stages of dementia or near the end of life. A healthcare power of attorney gives the person of your choice, your agent or attorney-in-fact, the power to implement your healthcare wishes as outlined. Typically, this person should be a person you fully trust with your life, as they will be making the decision on whether to "pull the plug" or not.

Estate planning is specific to each jurisdiction. Any time you move to another state or province you should have your estate plan reviewed by a local attorney to ensure your plan is compliant with local estate laws. This is also true if you are moving to another country. You should also have your estate plan reviewed every five to 10 years to ensure that no revisions are needed due to changing estate and probate laws in your jurisdiction. Relationships also change, and the people you previously selected as power of attorney or executor may not match your current wishes. Attorneys often recommend your healthcare power of attorney be someone local. Once you move across the border for retirement, you will need to have a new estate plan created in your new home jurisdiction.

---

[127] https://www.investopedia.com/terms/p/powerofattorney.asp

Canadian estate planning is like U.S. estate planning in many ways, with some key differences. The documents used in Canada are very similar to those used in the U.S. The Canadian equivalent of the U.S.'s General Durable Power of Attorney is called the Power of Attorney for Property. Canada's version of the U.S.'s Healthcare Power of Attorney is the Power of Attorney for Personal Care, so very similar. Most Canadian estate plans consist of a will and the two power of attorney documents. Trusts are not as commonly used in Canada.

Canada is a less litigious society, so lawsuits are less common, and it is less common for a will to be challenged in probate. This is the main reason trusts are less common in Canada. The other reason is that trusts are taxed punitively. All trust income is taxed at the top federal and provincial marginal tax rate, usually 50% or more. Also, there is no such thing as a Revocable Living Trust in Canada. An RLT is a pass-through entity, so any income received by the trust is taxed to the owner personally. All trusts in Canada are a separate entity and are taxed as such. Any time funds are contributed to a trust, a deemed disposition takes place and the grantor must pay tax on all capital gains. The trust then has a basis of the market value at the time of contribution. All income is then taxed at the top marginal tax rate. U.S. trusts have their own tax schedule, with the top rate of 37% starting at $15,200 in 2024. As you can see, trusts are far less efficient in Canada.

If you are moving to the U.S., you need to do your estate planning with consideration of the Canadian non-resident trust rules. Any U.S. trust established within five years of the grantor (person contributing property) exiting Canada may be deemed by the CRA to be a Canadian trust and will be taxed as such. Even after five years, if any trustees are Canadian residents, the trust may be deemed a Canadian trust because the "mind and management" of the trust is in Canada. While taxes are always an important consideration, maintaining control and ensuring your wishes are carried out may be more important and justify using a trust.

When making this consideration, remember only the retained income is taxed to the trust. Distributed income is taxed at the personal level based on who receives it. Children are expensive and the guardians you select may need to make significant lifestyle changes (new home or vehicle) to accommodate additional children. For these reasons, a trust should not be ruled out simply because of the five-year "lookback" rules. Qualified Canada-U.S. legal counsel should be sought when doing your estate planning to ensure that cross-border elements are properly addressed.

When families establish trusts in Canada, it is usually for control purposes. This is often accomplished using testamentary trusts. A testamentary trust is one that is established through the will. In other words, no trust exists while you are alive. After you pass away, your will calls for the executor to establish a testamentary trust, which is a legal entity and becomes active at that time. The assets that are designated to the trust are transferred in and then administered according to the directives of the trust. This is commonly used in estate plans for families who have heirs who are minors, disabled, or are in another situation where it is not wise to give outright gifts of cash. This may be the case if an heir has an addiction, is pending divorce or is lawsuit prone. In this case, the benefit of control and protection may outweigh the punitive tax treatment. You can also simply distribute all the income and pay no tax at the trust level.

Once your last will, general durable powers of attorney and healthcare directives are created, your estate plan needs to be implemented. You should review your RRSPs, LIRA, IRA, and 401(k) to ensure they have a named primary and contingent beneficiary that is in line with your wishes. If you do not have a contingent beneficiary listed and both spouses pass away simultaneously, such as in a car accident, your retirement accounts will be paid to your estate and must go through probate before funds are paid to the beneficiary determined by the courts. This can cause delays with the release of funds needed to support your family. The implementation of your estate plan may also include gifting or retitling of accounts. If your estate plan involves the use of a trust, the funds will have to be transferred into an account in the name of the trust. There may be gifting that needs to be done, especially if you are moving to Canada and want to take advantage of income splitting.

Be sure you have a conversation with those involved in your estate plan to ensure they understand your wishes and the rationale behind them. You may want to outline their role in your estate plan and why you selected them. Ensure they are comfortable implementing your plan as you wish. If you desire the "plug to be pulled," emphasize to your healthcare agent(s) that, if that time should ever come, they should remember this conversation and take comfort in the fact that these are your wishes. This should also be specifically stated in your healthcare directives. Even more important is communicating the location of important documents so that your estate plan can be implemented in line with your wishes.

Overall, there are many different taxes that need to be considered at death, particularly at the passing away of the second spouse. These include estate taxes, income taxes, deemed disposition taxes, gift taxes, state inheritance taxes and generation skipping transfer taxes. These taxes range from 40% to 50% or more, and are in addition to any probate, court or attorney's fees your estate may incur during settlement. Currently in the U.S., you are each eligible to pass the exemption equivalent of $13.61 million (2025) on to your heirs tax-free. This does not include any income taxes.

Estate planning is easier for U.S. residents if both spouses are U.S. citizens. Moreover, when spouses are U.S. citizens, you eliminate the need for Qualified Domestic Trust (QDOT) provisions, and annual gifting is unlimited during your lifetimes. You will need to revise your estate plan again if your citizenship status changes. I recommend married couples become U.S. citizens if their intention is to remain in the U.S. permanently. There are not the same estate planning advantages to becoming Canadian citizens.

In 2025, every person is eligible to gift up to $19,000 USD per year to any one person, with no limit on the number of people gifted to. This should be kept in mind as your estate grows, or if the estate tax exemption level is decreased in the future. Passing your assets to your heirs does not have to wait until you are gone. This can begin earlier with cash gifts, or transfers into an irrevocable trust where there are some controls built in.

Gifts to non-citizen spouses are limited to $190,000 USD in 2025. Should you give a gift above the exemption level, you will have to file IRS Form 709 – *United States Estate (and Generation-Skipping Transfer) Tax Return* to report it. There is no tax due if your gift is below the estate and gift tax exemption amount, but filing the form will increase your tax preparation fees. The most common way I see non-citizens getting into trouble with gifting is through transferring assets between spouses above the gifting limit, including moving assets into joint accounts and real estate into joint ownership. You are eligible to pay tuition or medical expenses directly to the institution for anyone and not have it count towards your annual gifting exemption. All education and medical expenses paid for your spouse, children, or grandchildren should go directly from your account to the institution.

There is no estate tax in Canada, but there is a death tax. The deemed disposition tax at death is a tax on any previously untaxed income. This includes your registered account balances (if passing to anyone other than your spouse), unrealized capital gains in your taxable accounts, unrealized capital gains in an real property other than your permanent residence, and appreciation in business value for the self-employed. Ontario also imposes a probate fee of $5 per $1,000 on the first $50,000 of assets subject to probate and $15 per $1,000 on the remaining assets. Each province has a similar probate fee schedule.

It is interesting to note that Section 70(3) of the Canada Tax Act allows an IRA to be treated as a "right or thing". A U.S. beneficiary of an IRA owned by a Canadian tax resident does not have to pay income tax on the IRA distributions and the IRA is not included in the deemed disposition upon death. It is a common filing position that an IRA is a "right or thing".

There are three options upon death for a right or thing:

- Include the value of the IRA in the deceased's income in the year of death.
- File a separate return to report the right or thing in the year of death.
- Transfer the IRA to beneficiaries using 70(3) of the Canada Tax Act.

If you have non-resident beneficiaries, your executor should choose option three and the IRA would avoid future taxation in Canada. Option three is still helpful for Canadian beneficiaries because it will give them an additional 10 years of tax deferral.

Finally, your financial plan should be looked at in totality, including immigration planning, customs planning, cash-flow planning, tax planning, retirement planning, risk management, education planning, investment planning and estate planning. The focus of this book is on planning your cash flows for retirement. Taxes and estate planning need to be taken into consideration as they affect your cash flows and asset ownership structure. Specifically, this comes into play if you have successful children and grandchildren who are in high tax brackets. Many parents work incredibly hard to make sure their children can go to law school, medical school or graduate school, or are in some other way set up for success. Generational wealth preservation is important to most of these families. As such, your heirs' tax situation needs to be considered as you get into your later years.

11

Glossary

1. 401(k) – Tax-deferred, employer-sponsored, qualified retirement plan.
2. 403(b) - Like a 401(k) but for government employees.
3. 529 Education Savings Plan – Education savings account available in the U.S. that allows for tax-free growth if distributions are used for qualified education expenses.
4. AAII – Adjusted aggregate investment income - The income earned through investments made within a corporation, such as dividends, interest, rent, and 50% of capital gains is considered passive investment income, also known as adjusted aggregate investment income (AAII) for tax purposes.
5. ACA – Affordable Care Act – The "Affordable Care Act" (ACA) is the name for the comprehensive health care reform law (passed in 2010) and its amendments. The law addresses health insurance coverage, health care costs, and preventive care.
6. AGI – Adjusted Gross Income – Gross income minus some deductions.
7. AMT – Alternative Minimum Tax - The alternative minimum tax (AMT) applies to taxpayers with high economic income by setting a limit on those benefits. It helps to ensure that those taxpayers pay at least a minimum amount of tax.
8. AUM – Assets Under Management – The amount of assets an advisor or

firm is managing.

9. Beneficiary – The person to receive funds if the account owner dies.

10. BL – Business Limit – The federal business limit is $500,000 for 2009 and later years.

11. CAD – Canadian dollars

12. Cash-Flow Sequencing – The sourcing of cash for living expenses from different types of accounts in retirement.

13. CCPC – Canadian-Controlled Private Corporation – Corporate structure used by high-income and self-employed Canadians to control tax liability.

14. CD – Certificate of Deposit – A type of savings account that pays a fixed interest rate on money held for an agreed-upon period.

15. CDA – Capital Dividend Account - A special corporate tax account that gives shareholders designated capital dividends, tax-free. When a company generates a capital gain from the sale or disposal of an asset, 50% of the gain is subject to a capital gains tax. The non-taxable portion of the total gain realized by the company is then added to the capital dividend account (CDA), which is then distributed to shareholders.

16. CDC – Centers for Disease Control and Prevention – U.S. federal agency that protects the public from various health related threats.

17. CDSB – Canada Disability Savings Bond - The grant is an amount that the Government of Canada pays into a registered disability savings plan (RDSP). The government will pay a matching grant of 300%, 200% or 100%, depending on the beneficiary's adjusted family net income and the amount contributed.

18. CDSG – Canada Disability Savings Grant - The grant is an amount that the Government of Canada pays into a registered disability savings plan (RDSP). The government will pay a matching grant of 300%, 200% or 100%, depending on the beneficiary's adjusted family net income and the amount contributed.

19. CESG - Employment and Social Development Canada (ESDC) provides an incentive for parents, family and friends to save for a child's post-secondary education by paying a grant based on the amount contributed

to a registered education savings plan (RESP) for the child. The Canada education savings grant (CESG) money will be deposited directly into the child's RESP.

20. CFA – Chartered Financial Analyst – The premier international investment management designation.

21. CFC – Controlled Foreign Corporation – A foreign corporation owned or controlled by a domestic person.

22. CFP® - Certified Financial Planner – The premier financial planning designation.

23. CIM – Chartered Investment Manager – Minimum required education standard to be registered as a portfolio manager in Canada.

24. COBRA – Consolidated Omnibus Budget Reconciliation Act – Allows former employees to keep their health insurance for up to 18 months after severing service from an employer.

25. Coinsurance – The portion of an expense paid by the insured rather than the insurer.. COLA – Cost of Living Adjustment – Annual increase in pension benefits usually based on the CPI

26. Copayment – The amount paid by the insured anytime there is an insurance claim.

27. Covered Expatriate – Former U.S. citizen or permanent resident who gave up their immigration status with the U.S. and otherwise qualifies as a Covered Expatriate.

28. CPA – Certified Public Accountant – The premier tax designation.

29. CPI – Consumer Price Index – A measure of the increase in the cost of goods and services over time.

30. CPP – Canada Pension Plan – Contributions-based public pension for all workers in Canada.

31. CRA – Canada Revenue Agency – Canadian tax collection agency for federal taxes.

32. DB – Defined Benefit Plan – qualified employer-sponsored retirement plan where the employer is the primary contributor and the retirement benefit is defined for the employee. The investment risk lies with the employer.

33. DCP – Defined Contribution Plan – qualified employer-sponsored retirement plan where the employee is the primary contributor, sometimes with an employer contribution or match, and the retirement benefit is not defined for the employee. The investment risk lies with the employee.

34. Deemed Disposition – When unrealized capital gains are taxed when no sale occurred.

35. DPOA – Durable Power of Attorney – Remains in effect until the principal revokes the powers or dies.

36. DTC – Disability Tax Credit – Tax credit available to eligible taxpayers to offset expenses associated with the care of yourself of a dependent.

37. Employer Sponsored Retirement Plan – A qualified retirement plan sponsored through your employer.

38. Estate Tax – Tax levied on the assets in the estate of a deceased person.

39. ETF – Exchange Traded Fund – Pooled investment popular for low fees and tax efficiency.

40. Executor – Person charged with administering a Will.

41. Exercise/Strike Price – The price at which a stock option can be purchased by the holder.

42. Exit Return – The final tax return filed by those moving away from Canada.

43. Expatriation Tax – Tax paid upon exit from the U.S. by Covered Expatriates.

44. FBAR – Report of Foreign Bank and Financial Accounts – Per the Bank Secrecy Act, every year you must report certain foreign financial accounts, such as bank accounts, brokerage accounts and mutual funds, to the Treasury Department and keep certain records of those accounts.

45. FICA Taxes – Payroll taxes for Social Security and Medicare.

46. FRA – Full Retirement Age – A term used to describe the age at which you can begin Social Security, Canada Pension Plan, Old Age Security, and other pension retirement benefits without a reduction in your benefit amount.

47. FX – Foreign (Currency) Exchange

48. General Limitation Foreign Tax Credits – Foreign tax credits created

from income that does not qualify as passive such as employment income.

49. GIC – Guaranteed Investment Contract – An agreement between an investor and an insurance company that guarantees a certain rate of return on an investment over a specified period.

50. GILTI – Global Intangible Low-Income Income - Global Intangible Low-Taxed Income is a minimum tax targeted at foreign earnings from intangible assets such as copyrights, patents, trademarks, etc. and was adopted when the U.S. moved from a worldwide tax system to a territorial tax system.

51. Government Retirement Pension Benefits – Social Security, Canada Pension Plan, Old Age Security.

52. Grantor – Person titling assets in the name of the trust.

53. Green Card Holder – U.S. Permanent Resident

54. Gross Rent – Total rents received.

55. Group RRSP – RRSP offered through an employer or other trade group.

56. HBP – Home Buyer's Plan - The Home Buyers' Plan (HBP) is a program that allows you to withdraw from your registered retirement savings plans (RRSPs) to buy or build a qualifying home for yourself or for a specified disabled person. Currently the HBP withdrawal limit is $60,000.

57. HDHP – High-Deductible Health Plan - A health insurance plan with a sizable deductible for medical expenses and relatively low premiums.

58. Healthcare Agent – Medical Power of Attorney – A person you allow to make decisions for you in case you can't make them yourself.

59. HSA – Health Savings Account - Tax-advantaged account created for or by individuals covered under high-deductible health plans (HDHPs) to save for qualified medical expenses.

60. Income Attribution Rules – Income from gifted funds or investments is attributed back to the person who gave the gift.

61. Inherited IRA – The type of IRA used when an IRA or other tax-deferred qualified retirement plan is inherited.

62. IRA – Individual Retirement Account – qualified, tax-deferred.

63. IRS – Internal Revenue Service – U.S. tax collection agency for federal taxes.

64. LIF – Life Income Fund – LIRAs must be rolled to a LIF by December 31 of the year the owner turns 71. Distributions must begin the following year with an annual minimum and maximum.

65. LIRA – Locked-In Retirement Account – Used for Canadian pension rollovers regulated provincially.

66. LLC – Limited Liability Corporation – A type of incorporation typically used by small businesses in the U.S.

67. LRIF – Like a LIF, only available in Newfoundland and Labrador, maximum distribution is calculated differently.

68. LRSP – Locked-In RRSP – Like a LIRA but for federal pensions.

69. MAGI – Modified Adjusted Gross Income – Adjusted gross income with some deductions added back in.

70. Market Correction – When the stock index average goes down by 20% or more.

71. MFJ – Married Filing Jointly (U.S.)

72. Minimum RRIF Amount – The amount that must be distributed annually beginning the year after an RRSP balance is transferred in.

73. NERDTOH – Non-Eligible Refundable Dividend Tax on Hand - The calculation of a private corporation's dividend refund is based on two accounts, the eligible refundable dividend tax on hand (ERDTOH) and the non-eligible refundable dividend tax on hand (NERDTOH).

74. Net Rent – Rent after taxes, expenses, depreciation, or capital cost allowance.

75. Net Worth – Assets minus liabilities

76. NIIT – Net Investment Income Tax - The NIIT applies at a rate of 3.8% to certain net investment income of individuals, estates and trusts that have income above the statutory threshold amounts.

77. No matter what your family income is, ESDC pays an amount of Canada Education Savings Grant (basic CESG) of 20% of annual personal contributions you make to all eligible RESPs for a qualifying beneficiary to a maximum CESG of $500 in respect of each beneficiary ($1,000 in CESG

if there is unused grant room from a previous year), and a lifetime limit of $7,200.

78. NR-73 – The form the CRA uses to determine residency status.

79. NYSE – New York Stock Exchange – the primary exchange or platform on which most public U.S. stocks trade.

80. OAS – Old Age Security – public pension for all qualifying residents in Canada. Earned through residency rather than contributions.

81. OAS Clawback – Means tested tax on OAS benefits.

82. Obamacare – Nickname for the Affordable Care Act because it was passed while President Obama was in office.

83. OSFI – Office of the Superintendent of Financial Institutions - Independent agency of the Government of Canada with a mandate to regulate and supervise more than 400 financial institutions and 1200 pension plans.

84. Passive Foreign Tax Credits – Foreign tax credits created from passive income such as capital gains, dividends, and interest.

85. Pension Adjustment – RRSP room is reduced by pension contributions.

86. PFIC – Passive Foreign Investment Company - A foreign corporation is deemed to be a PFIC if 75% or more of its gross income is from non-business operational activities. It would also qualify as a PFIC if at least 50% of its average percentage of assets are held for the production of passive income.

87. POA – Power of Attorney – A legal authorization that gives the agent or attorney-in-fact the authority to act on behalf of an individual referred to as the principal.

88. Premium Tax Credits – Means-tested tax credits applied to health insurance premiums for policies purchased through the healthcare exchanges.

89. Primary Residence Exemption – A tax exemption available, but structured differently in Canada and the U.S., on capital gains on your primary residence.

90. Probate – The legal process that assets of a deceased person go through to be distributed.

91. QCD – Qualified Charitable Distribution – Distribution made to charity rather than taken personally. The advantage is there is no income tax paid personally or by the charity resulting in a larger charitable contribution.

92. QDOT – Qualified Domestic Trust – A special kind of trust that allows taxpayers who survive a deceased spouse to take the marital deduction on estate taxes, even if the surviving spouse is not a U.S. citizen.

93. Qualified accounts – U.S. retirement savings accounts that are either tax-deferred or tax-free such as 401(k)s and Roth IRAs.

94. RDSP – Registered Disability Savings Plan – Savings account available to those who qualify for the Disability Tax Credit. Qualifying beneficiaries may also be eligible for the Canada Disability Savings Grant and the Canada Disability Savings Bond.

95. RDTOH – Refundable Dividend Tax on Hand - It is an accumulation of the refundable portion of Part I tax and Part IV tax payable, less any dividend refund received.

96. Reentry Permit – Permit allowing U.S. Green Card holders to re-enter the U.S. after living abroad.

97. Registered Accounts – Canadian retirement savings accounts that are tax-deferred and allow deductible contributions.

98. RESP – Registered Education Savings Plan - A registered education savings plan (RESP) is a contract between an individual (the subscriber), the Minister designated for the purposes of the Canada Education Savings Act, and a person (the promoter). Under the contract, the subscriber names one or more beneficiaries (the future student(s)) and agrees to make contributions for them, and the promoter agrees to pay educational assistance payments (EAPs) to the beneficiaries.

99. Returning Resident Visa – Visa allowing former U.S. Green Card holders to return to the U.S. to live.

100. RLT – Revocable Living Trust – Common type of Grantor Trust in the U.S. that is a pass-through tax entity and is revocable.

101. RMD – Required Minimum Distribution – The minimum distribution required annually from qualified retirement plans, currently starting by

April 1 following the year the owner turns 73.

102. Rollover IRA – The type of IRA used when a 401(k), 403(b), or other tax-deferred employer sponsored qualified retirement plan is rolled to an IRA.

103. Roth 401(k) – Tax-free 401(k) with non-deductible contributions.

104. Roth IRA – Tax-free qualified retirement savings plan with non-deductible contributions.

105. RRIF – Registered Retirement Income Fund – All RRSPs must be converted to RRIF accounts by December 31 or the year the owner turns 71. Minimum distributions begin the following year.

106. RRSP – Registered Retirement Savings Plan – Tax-deferred Canadian retirement account with deductible contributions.

107. SBD – A reduction in corporate taxes for CCPCs. The reduced rate of tax is available on active business income up to the corporation's business limit for the year.

108. SEC – Securities and Exchange Commission – The U.S. federal agency that oversees securities trading and federal advisor registration.

109. SEP IRA – Self-employed Person IRA – An IRA for those who are self-employed.

110. SIMPLE IRA – Savings Incentive Match Plan for Employees – Type of IRA for small businesses.

111. Solo 401(k) - 401(k) for self-employed individuals with no employees.

112. Spousal Benefit – Benefits available to the spouses of pensioners.

113. Spousal RRSP – RRSP available to spouses of those who have RRSP room. The spouse with the RRSP room makes the contribution into their spouse's account and the contributing spouse gets the deduction.

114. SS – Social Security – Contributions-based public pension system for most workers administered by the Social Security Administration in the U.S.

115. SSA – Social Security Administration – The agency that administers Social Security benefits.

116. SSDI – Social Security Disability Income – Disability income benefits from Social Security.

117. Substantial Presence Test – The test used to determine if a U.S. visit has been physically present in the U.S. long enough to be considered a U.S. tax resident. Failing the Substantial Presence Test and becoming a U.S. tax resident does not give anyone legal immigration status.
118. Tax Credit – Directly reduces tax liability.
119. Tax Deduction – Reduces taxable income.
120. Tax Drag – The amount taxes reduce a portfolio.
121. TFSA – Tax-Free Savings Account – Savings account available to all Canadian taxpayers with non-deductible and tax-free growth.
122. Trustee – The person who controls the property of a trust.
123. TSX – Toronto Stock Exchange – where most Canadian stocks trade.
124. ULC – Unlimited Liability Corporation – A type of incorporation typically used by small businesses in Canada.
125. USD – U.S. dollars

12

Author Contact

Lucas Wennersten, CFA, CFP® (Canada), CFP® (U.S.A.)

49th Parallel Wealth Management

info@49thparallelwealthmanagement.com

Canada Phone: (647) 670-1203

U.S. Phone: (480) 520-7770

9375 E. Shea Blvd., Suite 113D, Scottsdale, AZ 85260

www.49thparallelwealthmanagement.com

About the Author

You can connect with me on:

🌐 https://49thparallelwealthmanagement.com

f https://www.facebook.com/profile.php?id=61569377636962

🔗 https://www.youtube.com/@LucasWennersten

🔗 https://www.linkedin.com/in/lucas-wennersten-cfa-cfp%C2%AE-canada-cfp%C2%AE-u-s-a-5aa48147

Subscribe to my newsletter:

✉ https://mailchi.mp/49thparallelwealthmanagement.com/book-contacts